A Nobleman from Khorasan

Khalilullah Khalili

Translations by

M.F. Moonzajer

ISBN: 9781797991061

Table of Contents

(1)

KASA BURJ, THE PALACE OF PRINCESS

It was the seventeenth of Ramadan; the month Muslims fast for purity and nobility. The golden rays of the sun had climbed over the Chinari Mountain. It was a season of harvesting. Fruitful, sallow and plane trees had veiled under emerald leaves. Kandahari grapes had ripped, while other types of grapes were still green.

Grief and mourning were felt everywhere in Kabul. Maybe, the city expected a tragedy. Balahisar, a key for conquering Afghanistan was seized by the malicious enemy. Only two gates into the Balahisar, snatched by long spearheads of the vicious enemy were open for the commute. The first gate located at sunrise of Kabul, connecting Mastan Bridge to Shah Shahid main road. The second gate crossed a grandiose tomb connecting Balahisar to a public cemetery.

It was early morning and Kabul Bazaar was quiet like a dead; maybe, it was Ramadan, the month, Muslims avoid eating and drinking from dawn till sunset.

Yaqoob Khan; a wasted and sick king who inherited the throne, lived in the north of Kabul city in a walled castle. Everyone hoped he was alone in this savagery, but his reckless and unconscious ministers and friends lived with him too in the castle. His friends and administers only thought about their own greed.

Tremors of the Afghanistan army marches were heard time to time from Sherpoor Barracks. The king had ordered his generals to use the army of spear holders, gunmen, and artillery only for the purpose of defending the sovereignty of his country against all enemies. They must avoid going into wars by all means.

Men, women, and children scowled at beardless, long hairy mustached soldiers in the city. Anger had boiled inside the bone and blood of every citizen. They believed the soldiers holding guns and patrolling all over the city were like walking deaths;

their blood had frozen like zombies, and their souls were lifeless in their muscles.

The sound of the enemy horses hoofed in every lane of Kabul. Many people in the city fought and died, and many shed tears with broken hearts. Soldiers in Sherpoor barracks muffled, maybe they feared death. The King was sick, and his friends and advisors shamelessly circled his shaky throne like hyenas. They did not show bravery and devotion to their country and King. They were traitors. Their greed had overcome their patriotism; because they were promised wealth by the enemy. They were snakes in the sleeve.

The Palace of the princess had tall walls and four steel towers. In every tower, a beautiful mansion was built for embellishment. Gigantic black gates of the castle were made from pure steel and oversize colorful nails on the gate had added to its solemnity in the city.

Yards of the castle were decorated with sallow trees, flowers, and colorful paths. Spring was the best season in the castle. The fruitful trees grabbed every soul that put a step inside the castle and the muddy Kabul River crossed along the castle like a mad thunderstorm.

Several days passed. The queen and female slaves of the King's courtyard had left Sherpoor to visit the ill king in the castle. Male servants and gatekeepers guarded the palace against any unauthorized intrusion. The queen had asked Gul Chehra to supervise the palace and oversee the female slaves. Gul Chehra was also the instructor of the princess. The queen went to care for her husband. Gul Chehra spent scorching hot days with thirst and hunger in southwest tower, where she could watch Balahisar from the tower.

The northern tower was cozy and comfy. She could stay in there and breathe fresh air and watch Sherpoor; the house of the king, but she preferred staying in the southwest tower. She wanted to watch Balahisar, the camp of the enemy. It was a tragic day for the nation. The country needed its king the most, but the illness had crippled the king.

The enemy had crossed seas and mountains. They had come from Great Britain. Marches of their army had ignited anger and vengeance in every home. The gatekeepers and tower guards of the ill king were too weak to face an empire. The guards showed no hatred or anger against the enemy. Balahisar looked like a swollen heart from the colorful windows of the tower to Gul Chehra. She felt pain like an amputated soldier who could no more defend the line against the the enemy. Balahisar was the heart of Afghanistan, and walls along Lions Gate Mountains were like veins pulling the heart together.

The main gate located at the sunset of Balahisar. It connected snout of high mountains to the castle and the Kasa Burj was built on it. Women in the city called it Yak Lagho. Yak Lagho is a bowl like a plate with metal beak and a long handle. Some people call it "Bi Jan Jo", the abbreviation for a British soldier who guarded this gate and was slaughtered by people during the uprising. It had many names, but everyone knew it by Kasa Burj. The ancient wall attached to Lions Gate Mountains was like a thirsty dragon, plunging its head onto a plate.

The wall had curves and twists. Another similarity of the wall to a dragon was the bones of innocent people used as stone and bricks during ancient eras. In the ancient era, when labor could not work anymore, they used them as bricks to build walls. Human skulls were still visible on the wall. On the south of Kasa Burj, a cemetery was constructed for heroes. They called it the True Martyrs cemetery.

It was a sacred name!

Many believed that today was the last day for the sun to shine on the glory of Balahisar, the wall of Mizrab Shah and tower of Qotb Haider. Mizrab Shah and Qotb Haider were heroes of Kabul which the places were named after them. They had become legends for generations. The enemy aimed destroying everything.

The lavish and luxurious palaces of Moghuls and Abdalis still kindled bright. A roaring stream touched the chest of Mastan Bridge. Maybe the river wanted to overcome the bridge and conquer the city. The turquoise enameled Palaces of Hamayon; the Emperor of Moghuls on the south of Balahisar still shined brilliance during full moon nights.

Gul Chehra lived her life single and alone, but she had earned a place for herself in the palace. Her pride and character did not allow her to sacrifice her position for the company of a man. The city was under siege. Gul Chehra spent the day in the tower starring at Kasa Burj and Balahisar. She was not in danger, but she was worried about people in the city.

It was a sunny summer day, and scorching warmth of sun increased as every minute passed. Screams and shrieks were heard from the city. It was heroic voices of the brave men who crushed the dust and mist with their clamors. A soldier from Sherpoor garrison left his camp and ran towards Balahisar. It was a terrifying event.

Furious cavalries and infantries marched towards Balahisar to conquer camps of the enemy. What had happened that to the lazy soldiers who slept until midday and now suddenly marched like crazy gladiators? The crowd carried messages of morality, unity, and liberty with them. The soldiers were emotional and it made them unstoppable. It was an extraordinary moment that even stones, trees and soil moved with the crowd.

The enemy locked all gates to Balahisar and formed a line of soldiers with spears around the castle. Sky turn partially cloudy, but Gul Chehra still could see the exhibition from the tower. Women and girls climbed up on roofs of their house and felt the scorching sun on their back as clouds moved away. Everyone aimed for one goal; the goal of defeating foreign enemies. Choices were limited; death or freedom.

In a matter of minutes, gunmen joined and reinforced the spearmen to counter the crowd. The enemy knew if the crowd reach Kasa Burj, they would conquer Balahisar and annihilate them. Another division of Sherpoor soldiers arrived at Kasa Burj from Kharabat lane. Soldiers surrounded the enemy from two sides; Mastan Bridge and outskirt of Kasa Burj.

The enemy started firing at soldiers from over the walls of Kasa Burj. Soldiers on the ground still approached the walls. They sang songs of freedom and independence. Fires of bullets from guns, spears from hands, smoke from runs, and dust from muns darkened the day. Gunpowder and blood were mixed.

Gul Chehra saw everything. Brave soldiers quickly outnumbered the enemy and sprinted towards Kasa Burj. The battle was bloody and dangerous. Stones, spears, and bullets fell from every corner of the castle on brave soldiers, but they kept climbing up the walls. Many soldiers bled, and many died falling back on the ground. The songs for freedom and independence got even louder. The relentless and cruel enemy stood pitiless because they knew Kasa Burj was the strategic stand and the key in conquering Balahisar.

Soldiers were wounded and kept falling from over the walls to the ground. It was an overwhelming demonstration of how badly they wanted freedom. The enemy commander ordered his men to throw coins of silver and gold to distract the soldiers and create a diversion among them. The trick did not work. Nothing could stop them. Blood boiled in their veins and they were prepared to accept the death. Bullets, spears, and stones were accompanied by gold and silver, but the battle was thriving. The victory was imminent and nothing could change the fate.

Gul Chehra saw people in white clothes with sharp swords joining soldiers. The battle was not over, and more people in black dresses joined the soldiers. Gul Chehra did not know who these people were. As the battle turned sacrificial, she learned people in white were men reinforcing the soldiers, and those in black girls and women of Kabul prepared to die for freedom. The enemy was defeated and soldiers broke their fast, they trusted in God and listened to his instructions. They knew time was important in every struggle. It is how nobles live.

(2)

AN EAGLE

A young boy like an eagle departed flocks of eagles amid rains of bullets and instants of death. He jumped from one stone to another and went back to the ground. He grabbed a mug of water and climbed up to Kasa Burj. The scorching hot sun had dried every single drop of water from brave soldiers and dehydrated them. Thirst had reached its peak, but it had not overcome anyone. The eagle gave a few drops of water to a soldier and moved to the next one.

The day and the bloody war were almost over. The enemy was defeated. Brave soldiers had conquered Kasa Burj, and the army of the enemy had vanished. The commander of the enemy army, Kio Nari did not want to surrender. He exploded Kasa Burj with gunpowder and ammunition, turning his soldiers into smokes and ashes.

Soldiers collected guns as spoils of war. Bodies of brave soldiers were brought down from over the mountain and walls. The bodies were kept under a tree until the next day to be buried with respect and dignity they deserved. The young boy, who ran towards the enemy fires, carried water and helped wounded soldiers, was still alive. They named him "Saqaw"; water carrier. It was the most rewarding name a soldier could achieve for his devotion and sacrifice.

Soldiers returned to the city and cared for wounded fighters. Among the wounded soldiers, many of them were prisoners of war. The British soldiers who survived the explosion and battle were cared for and treated with decency and respect. The war was over and there was no need for more violence and bloodshed. People from all over the city greeted soldiers and dinned with them. Lanterns were lit in roads and lanes of Kabul. The night was bright and colorful like a day. Towers in Palace of the princess were in total darkness; it appeared the queen had not returned from Sherpoor yet.

Saqaw and his friends entered the Palace. Gul Chehra who had seen strengths and bravery of the soldiers opened the gates and welcomed them. Female slaves and bondwomen greeted the soldiers at the Gate. Gul Chehra hailed Saqaw and his friends. Everyone had broken their fast, but Gul Chehra was still fasting. She broke her fast with drops of water from the mug of Saqaw. When her tongue touched the water, she felt chilling syrup of honey, mixed with rosewater in her mouth.

(3)

THE TENT OF GANDOMAK

The vicious and brutal army of Great Britain invaded Kabul from three sides to revenge the death of their soldiers. They had seized the capital and ruined Balahisar. The city was in absolute mourning. Patriot leaders from all over the country have gathered people in villages to fight the enemy and free the country.

The enemy turned Kabul into the slaughterhouse of innocent people. Streets and roads were red; many shot and left and many shot and dragged around the city. Friends and relatives of the ill king have convinced him to surrender and flee to India. A battalion of the British army planned to escort the King and his friends to India. The British army had installed tents for the King and his friends on a grain field of rice and wheat in Gandomak village.

Additional military camps were established around the King's tent to counter any surprise attack.

It was midnight and the weather was hot and difficult to bear it. Breeze rarely brought cold winds from the snow-covered mountains of Spingar. Two big tents were in the area. The flag of enemy waved at the top of tents. The first tent belonged to the British army, while the second one belonged to the puppet king of Afghanistan.

The two big tents were guarded by many small tents. The King was a prisoner. His guards and advisors spied for the enemy. The enemy feared that the Afghanistani soldiers might attack the camps and free the king. The sky was clear and the stars stared back with sorrow and grave. Giant luminescent spotlights were hanged on pillars of each tent making them visible from a far distance. Big bushy cypress trees appeared like armored soldiers. British cavalries had cut mane of their horses. They feared that the white shades may expose them to Afghanistani soldiers, and make them vulnerable during dark nights.

British cavalries had uniforms like their skin color. They were nervous, and their eyes dreadfully searched for Afghanistani soldiers. The nightmare of a bloody night had painted a tragic picture. The king was already captured, and the enemy took him where they go. It was not far gameplay. The King's friends and advisors have already sold their soul to the enemy for money and wealth, and those who had opposed were slaughtered.

Balahisar became a hill of ashes. Afghanistani soldiers were wiped out from Sherpoor, and once again it became a British camp. The enemy still feared the most. Great Britain had learned that the people of this nation would never stop. They will always fight for sovereignty and freedom and they will not listen to any king or emperor. Men, women, children, elders, farmers, laborers, literate, illiterate; they all fight against foreigners. They take order and lead whenever needed. They are kings and soldiers. In such a tragic day, when the city bled, even the poorest and weakest of all shined like a sword against the enemy.

It was midnight in Gandomak. The ill and imprisoned king was still awake. He sat on his throne and wondered about his horrifying fate. He was anxious and quiet. He had lost his dignity and pride among his people. His city drowned in tears, blood, and fire. His friends, ministers, and advisors betrayed him and had become puppets of the enemy. He was worried because he did not know what was coming next. What was about to happen to his children? Where will he be buried?

He did not have an answer to any of those questions.

A curtain of his tent was pushed away and opened. He saw his friends and advisors in luxurious costumes. Mini swords hanged from their shiny golden belts. Their silky mufflers, imperial turbans, well-combed beard, and smiling faces bothered him. They bent and bowed to the king. The king saw betrayal, fraud, and treachery in their eyes. They glowed from joy. They were promised wealth and fortune by the enemy.

One of the men broke the silence.

"His Majesty, the Great King,

We, as your servants, friends, ministers, and advisors have convinced Great Britain to release you from this prison and escort you to a beautiful territory like heaven, where you can happily live. It is a place where you can hunt lions, ride elephants, live in luxurious palaces, and spend magical nights like legends. "

The second man continued.

"His majesty,

You have always told us, heaven is where one has comfort and is free from work. We owe you this.

Our dear king,

You do not need to worry about rebels and lawless people. It is our responsibility to take care of them. Snowy and cold climate of Kabul will never bother you. All tensions and strains will go away forever."

The King had no answer. He stared anxiously at his roof and laid his right hand over his sword. The sword he had never used it in his lifetime. His friends and advisors were mute and waited for his response.

The curtains were pushed away once again. Three men in military uniforms entered the tent without permission. Friends and advisors of the king stood up with pale faces; bent and bowed to the men. As every second passed, the king learned that things were getting worse. The first man who entered the tent appeared to be a high-ranking official, while the other two men had leather hats with a small sharp fluke on them. A shiny thin sword hanged on the officer's belt. He had black shiny boots, and a brazen chain attached his hat to his check. Blue collar and stars on his chest described him as a commander. His eyes were blue like a cat and sharp like a wolf demonstrating his brutality and cruelty.

The forty-five years old commander shook the king's hand with arrogance and sat in front of him. The sad king laid back silently.

"Her Majesty, the Queen; the chief commander of seas and lands has given me the privilege to deliver her message to you, king Amir Mohammad Yaqoob Khan, son of Amir Sher Ali Khan, the honorable king of Afghanistan."

The Brit continued.

"Her Majesty, the Queen has ordered us to take you to India; where you can happily and freely live under the protection of the Great Britain Empire. The Queen believes you are innocent, and we are committed to bringing your children, wives, and anyone you would like to accompany you safely with you. Her Majesty, the Queen will only undertake this commitment if you sign this agreement. Your friends and advisors accompanying you right now have expressed their consents about the contents of this agreement.

The translator made a Dari copy from the English and submitted both copies to the king. The translation was ratified by the Great Britain officer. The king grabbed the agreement and tried to read it by using his lantern lights. His hands trembled. The king in an irritated voice said.

"You have no right to take away the independence of my country and forcefully escort me to a foreign country. How would you expect me to sign such a shameful treaty that deprives freedom from my people and independence from my nation?"

The black-eye Afghans and blue-eye Brits gazed at each other signaling treachery and deception. His friends and advisors slowly approached the king and offered him their advice.

"Dear King, as your loyal friends, we believe there is no way, but signing this treaty. If you do not sign this agreement, it means everyone including your family and friends will be killed."

The king's hands trembled like a naïve leaf against a strong storm. He tapped his fingers over his sword handle and paused for a few seconds. He put the treaty on his desk and signed it. His friends and advisors cheered, applauded, and signed the treaty as witnesses. It was close to dawn. The sky was blue and the morning ended silently in Gandomak village. The tents of the enemy were gone from the Gandomak village.

(4)

A DAUGHTER OF BAMYAN

Her childhood was filled with love and affection in her parents' house. Her mother loved her and her father cared for her. It was everything she ever needed. She knew that she could run to her mom and seek shelter anytime. She was not afraid of thunderstorms, earthquakes, snow-hills, and flood. Her mother kept her safe! She asked her mother "Hug me and hide me in your arms". No place was safer than her mother's arms for her. She could spend the harshest days and nights in her arm without any fear. Her mother's arms were the safest place for her. She stayed over her bed late nights, sang and whispered her favorite lullaby.

"My love for you is immortal and forever

Like the lonely nights without mornings,

With those beautiful smiles and sweet frowns

When you look at me, I taste sweetness on my lips"

Gul Chehra still felt the warmth of her mother's kisses on her cheek and forehead. She could remember the beautiful story of the two big idols her mother had told her.

The giant idol was named Salsal, while the smaller Shah Maha. Salsal was the son of Jahan, the wrestler of Bamyan, while Shah Maha was the daughter of Mir of Amir River. Salsal was the bravest and strongest wrestler that ever lived. Shah Maha was a symbol of beauty and courage.

Once upon a time, Salsal saw Shah Maha and fell in love with her. The feelings were mutual. Shah Maha loved his bravery and heroism. The story of Salsal falling in love with Shah Maha became a tale across Bamyan and Amir River. Mir of Amir River did everything to postpone the matchmaking of Salsal and Shah Maha. Nevertheless, inevitably he put forward his conditions for the engagement.

"A blockage must be built against the Amir River. Whenever the water rises, it must not destroy and wash out the people's farms. It must also help people and crops in times of drought. Wild tigers that have created fear and panic among people must be stopped and killed.

And finally, the two-head dragon, which has burned and killed forty innocent girls with his flaming breaths, must be hunted down. Once these conditions are met, Salsal can marry Shah Maha. "

Salsal spent three years to build the blockage. He killed the wild beasts and tigers. He hunted down the two-head dragon by the sword made of ancient steel. He ordered the men to make carpet from the skin of the dragon for his beloved. Because of his accomplishments, Bamyan and the Amir River area were as green and auspicious as heaven.

People were happy. They dreamed about the wedding day. They decorated the entire city by flowers to express their gratitude for Salsal and Shah Maha. The groom was a symbol of bravery, and the bride was a symbol of beauty and morality among people. Everyone joined the ceremony to celebrate. The elders in Bamyan and the Amir River requested their people to carve two monuments honoring the bride and the groom.

Everyone welcomed the recommendations and carved two monuments. The first one was carved by people of Bamyan in honor of the bride, and the second one, by the people of Amir River in honor of the groom. It was proposed that the groom must stand next to the monument built by the bride's people, and the bride stand next to the monument built by the groom's people. People of Bamyan and Amir River will stand in lines and praise the marriage.

Nowroz (The New Year festival) was celebrated with profuse magnitude than ever before. Spring arrived. The next morning, the bride and the groom appeared in elegant dresses together, and the beautiful morning breeze added to their beauty. The branches of almond and apricot trees became colorful with blossoms. The beautiful blue sky and the chirping of birds from over the stones, and walls gave strengths to every soul. Brindled fish jumped and played on waves of silver like streams and lakes, the spots on their skins seemed like seeds of ruby, igniting charm and magic.

Gazelles with tall warped horns and leaping deer with small horns moonlike jumped and ran in circles across the green field. In the chest of mountains range, three lines were drawn like a cloth of beautiful silk; a vivid white line along the snow-covered castles, a green emerald line along the thick trunk of green forests, and a red twilight line along the tulip's lawns. It felt like life and love breathed inside every object; stones, flowers, and trees whispered to each other. Every drop of water and every bit of soil felt joy and happiness.

Salsal was covered with a curtain made of colorful

silk, and Shah Maha was covered with a curtain made of soft green silk. The plan was to push away the curtains when the sun rises, so the people could see the brave man of Bamyan, Salsal, and the angel of Amir River, Shah Maha for the first time. They wanted to send waves of happiness across mountains and seas. The curtains were pushed away, a thousand hearts and eyes that beat like mills, and never blinked, suddenly were shocked and silenced.

It was the silence of death and the shock of horror. Yes, both lovers had turned into stone.

They were stones, yes soundless stones; cold and breathless. People bent and bowed from fear and horror. From that day onward Bamyan has named the temple of love. People decided to mourn one night every week for two failed lovers.

Gul Chehra quoted his mother

"This is the secret of the temple of love, and the city of screams (Gholghola[1]). "

Whenever Gul Chehra thought about her childhood friends, tears fell from her almond shaped eyes. She

____

[1]City of Screams is 13th century city in Bamyan, Afghanistan which was conquered by Genghis Khan after months of surrounding.

felt pain. The clapping of her father's horse always awakened her from slumberland. She could remember the days when her father put her on horseback and carried her across the rivers, and forests… She was always loved and cheered more than her siblings. She whimpered and mourned those days now.

(5)

A BROTHERHOOD PACT

Saqaw and his friends were covered in blood when they returned from the bloody Kasa Burj battle. They were exhausted and after being welcomed by Gul Chehra they slept like knights in the palace; quiet and with confidence.

The chirping of birds and cockcrows of roasters awakened Saqaw and his friends. He and his friends went to visit Balahisar and Kasa Burj. The mourning was not over. They had to bury the brave soldiers and pray for their souls. They were left in the graves with their clothes and buried barefoot side by side like a family. Children and parents shed tears and cried for their beloved ones. Mothers mourned for their sons, and they were proud of them. People brought flowers and left them on the grave of soldiers.

The cemetery extended from Shrine of Shah Shahid to Lal Jaba Buland Kaman and from Khoja Roshnayi to Khoja Safa.

Balahisar was covered with fire and smoke. The city smelled gunpowder and blood. People cared for the wounded soldiers of the enemy, provided them comfort, and punished the traitors who betrayed their own motherland and had joined the enemy. The few who betrayed the nation were shot along the Balahisar wall, and their dead bodies were thrown in a deep trench of Balahisar.

No one knew what that happened to the King and his wanton advisors.

The night was almost there and stars blinked in the sky. The moon shined and lit the graves of brave soldiers. People came in groups from all over the city and lit candles. The outskirts of mountains glared like a lightsome day at night. It was a glorious moment. People had seen candle lights and glares before when the king celebrated the princess's birthday, but people never felt proud as they did tonight.

Many believed that candle lights over the grave of a soldier are the cresset of God. It was the eighteenth of Ramadan and every got together and prayed. Mosques were filled with worshipers. The nation was touched by the sacrifice and devotion for freedom. It was an auspicious night for the martyrs as they present their soul to their God.

Gul Chehra invited Saqaw and his friends for dinner. Saqaw was known as Baba (father) among his friends. The candle lights were pallid in the chamber of guests in the palace. Lala and his friends had scarves wrapped around their waist. The bony handle of a sharp blade was visible on Saqaw's waist. He appeared stronger and muscular.

His Mashk, (the bottle of water) he carried during the wars was hanged on the wall. The soldiers leaned their guns on the wall next to them. Dinner was served and the soldiers begged permission to leave. Gul Chehra gave a handkerchief full of sweets and dried fruits to every soldier.

Gul Chehra told Baba that his bravery and courage was heroic and it has become a legend among bondwomen in the palace. Baba thanked and expressed his gratitude for the good words. Gul Chehra hesitantly asked him if he would consider her to be his sister. Baba smiled and accepted the invitation. Gul Chehra insisted that now it is the duty of a brother to visit her sister and inquire about her wellbeing. Baba and his friends left the palace and headed towards his homeland to meet his people.

(6)

A STORYTELLER

In a light blue-sky night, stars gazed back with humor and remorse. The Queen's bed was decorated with silver and precious items on the terrace of the Palace. She often lay back in her soft satin bed and flowers around her bed perfumed the air. Silence governed the terrace and her chamber. Two bondwomen massaged the palm of her feet. She had a big bottle of fruit juice on a table next to her bed.

Gul Chehra was in her fifties. She sat next to the Queen and constantly waved a handy fan made of peacocks' feather to bring fresh air and give the queen comfort. The waves of the fan-created sways on the queen's hair.

Like all the other slaves, Gul Chehra had lost all her feminine feelings and wishes within the walls of the palace. She was a sculpture carved from a stone with no feelings, emotions, freedom or will. She was a thing among other properties of the King and Queen.

The Queen laid her head back on a fluffy pillow attired with golden buttons and waited for Gul Chehra to tell her a story like every night.

Gul Chehra intuited.

"I am bored of telling tales of Amir Hamza and 1001 nights… I am going to tell her a new story tonight."

Gul Chehra was not feeling well and it was difficult for her to not sleep at all. She tried to remember a new story that she had not told the Queen before, but her mind did not favor her. She decided to tell the Queen, her (Gul Chehra) own story. Gul Chehra's life was an untold story and the queen really liked new stories.

"Once upon a time, there was a small village on outskirts of a high mountain. The mountain was covered with forest trees and snow. The village had a fort as high and gigantic as the Palace of Princess. The fort belonged to a farmer who had many sheep and horses. People respected him as the father of their tribe. She had a daughter, as beautiful and stunning as an angel. Her father loved her more than he loved all her siblings. He took her to farm. He put her on the horseback and told her stories of their ancestors. Whenever the farmer ran into a teacher on their way, he asked him to teach her daughter how to read and write.

Her mother loved and adored her. Every morning, she woke her up with a kiss on the forehead and prayed for her safety and health. She hugged her for minutes, wished her to come home safely and then let her go with her father. Her mother made her a mascot for her safe return. The mascot was covered with leather and wrapped on a silver coin. She hanged it on her daughter's neck to keep her safe.

In summer, the temperature was high and she spent time with her father under shadows of a plane and sallow trees next to a river. The river provided chilling and fresh air. At nights, she slept next to her parents. She counted stars and played with them until she fell asleep. In winters, she laid back next to a window in her room where she could cover herself with a blanket. She watched the snow on their farm. She loved natural beautiful. Snowfalls in winter and tree blossoms in spring were her favorite theater.

Many people in the village also called her father Mir of Bamyan. Her daughter was dear to everyone in their village. As she grew up, she became a fairytale of beauty and prettiness. Her father stopped taking her to the farm, no matter how much she insisted on going with him.

Once upon a time her father went out for hunting but did not return as usual. The day became darker and the sun disappeared behind the snow-covered mountains. She was worried and fretted watching roads and waiting for her father return. She was frightened and could even hear her own heartbeats panting faster and faster every minute.

She walked ahead and looked closely for her father to appear from lanes of the forest covered with trees. She felt she was followed, but she could not see anything. She decided to go back to the fort and tell her mother that her father has not yet arrived. When she turned around two hands as strong as steel grabbed her tight, and locked her up. Her mouth and hands were tightened by black scarves in a matter of seconds and she was placed on the back of a horse.

She was a simple rural girl with an innocent soul and kind heart. She believed all humans are kind gentle and merciful. She kept quiet, smiled and ticked his head and neck with her little fingers. She hugged him from behind. The little girl became impatient and tried to unlock the knot from her eyes and mouth, but it was impossible for her little soft fingers and tightened hands.

The horseman speeded up and sounds of the hoof of the horse touched the stones and echoed in mountain valleys. The horse ran as fast as a bullet fire in a flower hill. She was in pain. She knew that her caring father would never let her suffer and feel pain. She was doomed. She was cursed to the fate of many other girls who she had heard about them from her mother.

She attempted to jump from the back of the horse, but the stonehearted butcher had tightened up her legs to the chest of the horse. After hours of the ride, the horseman stopped and put her on the ground. The stranger freed her hands, mouth, and eyes. The moment she saw the light, she found herself trapped among fearful and frightening narrow valley walled by two giant mountains.

A man stood up in front of her. He had long black boots and his face was covered with a red scarf. His gun was dangling around his shoulders. His coarse whip on his right hand was as frightening as a dark night. She cried and screamed, but in total darkness and far away from humanity, no one could hear her. She felt pain in her throat and barely could swallow her own saliva. She begged for mercy and cried in front of him.

The stranger in a hostile voice threatened her.

"If you scream or cry again, I will kill you. I will skin you alive and then give your body to beasts and wolves."

She kneeled, grabbed his feet, kissed his dusty boots, and begged him. Tears from her innocent eyes touched her dark brown hair and reached to the corners of her chain. A few drops of tear fell on the ground. It was an unbelievably heartbreaking moment that stones would have cracked, but the stonehearted stranger grabbed her hand forcefully and put her on the back of the horse. He squeezed and tied her legs to the chest of the horse. He covered her face with a black blanket, knotted her hands with a rope and speeded up.

The princess became a bait and a prisoner of a total stranger. She whimpered all the way… she could not move even an inch. She was like a weak lamb caught by a wild wolf, or a young pigeon hunted by a hungry eagle.

She was blindfolded. She could not see the light and did not know the sunset and sunrise. The only sound that accompanied her heartbeats was the hoof of the horse touching the ground. She knew she was far away from home and humans. Fear dominated her and she lost hope of getting back to the arms of her mother.

The stranger stopped the horse occasionally after a

few hours, put the girl on the ground, fed the horse, and tried to feed the girl with a mouthful of bread. It was the only time she could stretch her little feeble legs. The ground was full of barb bushes. Every time she looked in the sky and blinking stars, tears rounded up in her eyes and check. It reminded her beautiful mountains and blue sky of Bamyan.

She needed her mother to care for her wounds. She needed her brave father to save her from the cannibal beast. She needed her friends and help of people of Bamyan. She needed everyone's help. No one knew how long she was on this doomed journey. She was weakened and palled. Fever, hunger, thirst, and sleeplessness conquered her piece by piece.

Her chest had turned red. It was itchy. She was wounded and she barely could breathe air. Her legs and hands were powerless and breathless. Journey continued… she often fainted and laid on the shoulder of enemy…

(7)

FEELING SAFE

After spending many traumatizing nights on the back of a horse, she was awakened by a striking light. She could not see anything for a couple of seconds. She felt she was blind. Once the blurry images were gone; she felt safe seeing women around her. She assumed her mother was also there too.

"Mother! Mother!" She called.

She rubbed her eyes thinking she might be still asleep. Women around her who all shared the same fate, tried to help and comfort her, but there was no medicine in the world that could replace her mother. She had a fever for several days and felt exacerbating pain. It took her a week to recover from wounds. She knew she was millions of miles away from home. She cried and suffered like a candle melting down inside an oven. She was a prisoner in a nightmarish castle surrounded by tall walls and terrifying abnormality. Big enabled buildings, bulky walls, colorful rugs and carpets, bizarre flowers and trees, strange faces, weird dresses, erratic foods and unusual names, titles, and dialogues; it appeared she was in a different planet; a planet where only slaves and lords existed.

It was a planet where right and wrong were defined by the owner and lord. It was a world where people were treated like objects. Slaves bent and bowed and walked with their heads down and their body like a snake crawled on the floor. They served the lords. Polished and cleaned their shoes, cooked, cleaned and served them continuously. They were sculptures. They stood up on their feet for hours and never trembled from thirst, hunger or cold. They only eat and drink when they were told.

Cursing, beating, whipping and locking up were common. She had heard stories from her mother, but she never thought they were real. She had heard that when girls get pregnant, the ruthless men abort the innocent souls by beating up the girls. It was very painful that many died from unbearable agony. Maybe her mother stilled prayed for her and made her talismans because the prison was not as horrible for her as it was in stories.

(8)

A MIGHTY LADY

After several distressing days, the poor girl was taken to meet the leader of the castle. She was called a Mighty Lady. The lady was a powerful and wise person. She leaned on her decorated soft silk throne. Her long-tressed hair swung around her shoulders. Her precious golden rings attracted the crowd from distance. Two bondwomen with feather fans stood alongside her. She had a green exquisite shawl around her arms.

Many slaves were standing up and waited for her command. The lady had aged and had fainted eyesight. She asked the girl to come closer. She checked her hands, feet, and body thoroughly. She felt she was a criminal and about to be punished for her crimes. Her hands trembled and her teeth scuffed like from fear. She looked at the ground.

"She is worth more than what I have paid. Give her a bath, clean her and find her new clothes. I have heard she can read. Tell the instructor to help her with her education. She is beautiful and seems to be from a noble family. She will have a special place in this castle."

It was not difficult for Gul Chehra to understand what was going on. Instead of punishing the monster, they paid him. She was sold like property. She was a slave. She must forget her dreams and die in this castle like a prisoner. She would never be able to see her kind mother and a caring father. She was deprived of beautiful mountains, snow-covered forts, chirping birds, the beautiful breeze of Bamyan and her childhood friends.

If she were in Bamyan, one day she would be buried in their village hills. Her grieving parents would come over her grave and cry. There would be flowers every spring and New Year on her grave. Now, the prisoner was in oblivion. It was too much sorrow and woeful moments for her. Her throat clogged and she wanted to scream, but then she learned she was over the bed of the queen and the queen was snoring.

(9)

FLOWER AND ROSEWATHER

It was the early hours of the night. Mountains, deserts, forests and even the city were roofed by snow. It appeared that Kabul and their people were hibernating. Small streams across streets were frozen like ice camps. All roads to the city were blocked. Perhaps, it was not only the snow but also camphor[2] that had made the city breathless and silent; except those who were wounded or their beloved ones were in pain. Rich enjoyed the luxury, and poor prayed for food. Many still believed that things will change and good days will come. Winter nights were lengthy, but not enough length for those who needed it. Those who were imprisoned had <u>nothing else, but prayer to spe</u>nd their nights.

[2] Camphor is a natural aromatic compound used in the manufacture of film and plastics and as an external medicinal preparation. It is often given to men to weaken their sexual activity.

The queen's chamber was spectacular. The bed located in the middle, while candles were lit at both sides of her bed. Colorful lights sparked from half-burned chestnut woods inside the fireplace and added to the beauty of the room. It was lively. Flickers in the fireplace disturbed the silence. Smokes from the chimney of the chamber emerged like a black dragon and flew to the infinite sky.

Pearlish snowflakes brought messages of blessing and happiness. Black smoke and ashes erupted from luxurious palaces and formed dark clouds. Thick velvet curtains on windows of the palace did not allow the cold weather to get in, or the cozy airs get out. Only the poor felt cold and hunger.

The queen used different perfumes. She appeared more like a pharmacist rather than a queen. She had two small silver scent perfume boxes in her chamber that released the perfume into the air. She used two additional different perfumes for her hair and body. The perfumes all mixed up and created an aromatic chamber.

Two big tableaus with golden frames were installed inside the chamber. The first tableau was a portrayal of a baby deer with an arrow in her chest, while her mother watched her. The ground was covered with blood. The second tableau was a portrayal of an almond tree with blossoms and a little girl attempting to catch the branches.

Gul Begum, the queen lay back in her bed and covered her legs with a blanket made of soft silk. The candle lights fascinated her seductive and beautiful face. She stared at the ceiling and waited for Gul Chehra to tell her a story. Gul Chehra added more woods into the fireplace. She had to keep the chamber warm. Gul Chehra had a difficult job. She had to tell her a new story every night. The story must be interesting and exciting. Once the queen fell asleep, Gul Chehra had to be prepared whenever the queen woke up. She watched the stars and the moon every night. They were her friends. She told them her secrets and cried watching them.

She dreamed about her father making a snowman from snow on their backyard. They had adorable sheep and a beautiful white horse. What hurt her most was the story of that doomed night, when she could not recognize the hands of a monster from the hands of her kind father.

She had spent forty years in the castle. She had heard stories for all those years from different people. Everyone shared the same fate. Gul Chehra had memories of wars, victories, defeats, and freedom living in this castle.

It was time to tell another story.

Once upon a time; there were rumors that a beautiful female dancer named "Gulab" came to Kabul from India. She created a spark in Kabul with her magical hands, and body. She had enchanting moves. She found a special place in everyone's heart. People were prepared to give up everything to attend one of her shows. Many traveled for days and nights from the north to see her magical moves. Many believed she conjured and summoned people from monasteries and mosques. Madrassa students even under strict religious beliefs preferred her show over the study and praying.

Gulab was a master in music and dance. She melted hearts and captivated viewers. When she danced, the waves of her skirt rhymed with feelings of the audiences. She could give her audience a seizure at their every heartbeat. Her music was like bait, hunting down everyone. Her glances were poisonous and lethal. She was an angel of music and dance. She knew how to add beautiful in her art.

Gul, a rich and handsome guy was famous for his taste of luxurious life. He knew how to win a girl's heart. He lived like a prince. He had many gardens and properties. He was one of the wealthiest young men in the city. His father was a rich merchant who passed two years ago. Gul had inherited everything. When Gul met Gulab for the first time, he fell in love with her. It was not one of his crazy fantasies of hump and dump. He adored her. He gave up on his properties to pay off for her shows. He lost his gardens and most of his properties. Gulab saw him in all her shows and learned about his devotion to her. Its unconditional love of Gul sparked a fire in Gulab's heart.

The love story of Gul and Gulab became a legendary tale. Gulab did not perform shows anymore. She disappeared from the public eye. She quit everything, except her guitar. She spent her time playing it. The family and relatives of Gul tried to convince him to give up on Gulab, but he did not.

" Your relationship with Gulab will destroy and defame your father and ancestors name. You will lose public respect, and no one will ever talk about your ancestors in a good way. "

Gul did not listen to anyone. He was in absolute love with Gulab. Many beautiful and pretty girls from noble families tried to convince him to leave Gulab and marry them, but he said no to all of them. He was a stubborn lover. After all, Gulab was in love with Gul too, but she had not agreed to marry him yet. Gul camped in front of her house, spent days and nights hungry and thirsty. Gulab observed everything. The extreme love and devotion and finally agreed to marry him.

Gul and Gulab were engaged. They had planned to marry next month on the 21st of Ramadan. Gul sold his remaining properties and gave the money to Gulab for buying wedding dress and jewelry.

Gulab was a precious creature. Anyone who attended her shows had feelings for her. Her magic was strong, but a true love between Gul and Gulab was even stronger. That unconditional love between two birds changed everyone's mind about Gulab. The two lovers melted as their love profoundly were growing up every day.

Fate suddenly changed everything. A prince of the King's court who had heard of Gulab came between the two lovers. He wanted Gulab for himself, but people would oppose him because it was not acceptable. The prince sent his men after her. The guards broken into her house and seized her valuable belongings and took them to the palace. The men escorted Gulab to the Harem. The prince's men announced that she was brought to the harem to teach the slaves dancing and singing. They also circulated rumors that the prince favored his people by cleaning the city from devilry and dissipation. The king and his family were tyrants and no one could question them.

The incident was too severe for Gul to bear it. He turned to a demented and insane person. The prince's men exiled him from the city and sent him to the mountains and deserts to avoid any embarrassment to the prince. Everyone knew about Gul's true love for Gulab.

Gul crawled over mountains and deserts like snakes and scorpions. He was hungry, thirsty and had dirty clothes. He waited over the graveyards and sang the melody Gulab had taught him. He sang painful songs with sorrow and grief. Tears fell from his eyes like rain from a leaked sky.

One of his friends looked up for him for days. He finally found him over an old graveyard. He was beyond recognition. He seemed like a dead body raised from one of the graves. His face paled and blood had disappeared from his veins. He had dark yellow circles around his eyes. His beard and mustache were as chaotic as a jungle without animals. His lips dried and scorched like muds of a lake sprinkled from drought.

When Gul saw his friend, he ran towards him and hugged him firmly. He grabbed his hands and begged him to take him to the city and show him where they keep his Gulab. His friend could not refuse him. He took Gul with him back to the city.

It was spring season and the city blasted with tulips and colorful flowers. The breeze brought cool and fresh air and gave life to everything. His friend gave him a nice haircut and shaved his beard and mustache. He brought him to the castle. Gul saw men with spears and bats patrolling the castle. He went inside the castle and saw men with guns and firearms standing in lines.

He stared at tall walls touching clouds and Iron Gate turning the castle into a prison. He whispered to his friend. Have they imprisoned my Gulab in this cage? He lost consciousness and fell on the ground. The guards thought he might have been wrongly punished and tortured by someone, and has come to complain about it. The guards circled him. A noble scholar saw Gul and asked the guards to bring him to his chamber. The scholar, who was also the instructor of the prince helped Gul to recover and be able to speak again.

The scholar inquired about the poor man's situation and Gul told his story to him. Fear dominated the scholar. His hands trembled and his voice changed. He replied.

"Gulab is in Harem, a place we are not allowed to go. If I go there, the king will kill me."

Gul cried and whimpered. He grabbed the scholar's foot, begged and kissed his hands. The scholar pointed to Hafiz Shirazi's book lying on his desk and asked him to open a page from the book. Gul believed in fate and Hafiz Sherazi's poetry. He nodded his head as a sign of accepting the terms and opened the book. The first poem said.

Fate has decided for you, the flower and your rose,

One must be covered with curtains and one must be buried on the street.

Gul moaned from pain, coughed constantly and blood oozed from his mouth and nose. He leaned on the wall like a sculpture. The scholar approached him and checked his pulse. He was gone.

By mid-day, people carried two coffins to the cemetery. The second was Gulab's. She had a heart attack after hearing about Gul's fate. Gul Chehra looked at the queen. She had already fallen asleep.

(10)

A BASKET OF GRAPES

Many seasons passed. Days and nights elapsed like they never existed. Baba never broke the promise he made to Gul Chehra. Every year at the time of harvesting, he came to Kabul and visited Gul Chehra. He prepared baskets of grapes for sale in the city and made a special basket for Gul Chehra. He waited for the best time to travel. When the breeze blew, and the sun leaned below the beautiful mountains, Baba and his friends put the baskets on the back of their donkeys and traveled towards the city. They often reached Kabul by the dawn. It was a special season. Weather was nice, rivers were blue and the sky was shiny and full of stars. Beautiful mountains, entertaining rivers, long amusing nights and spacious deserts of Haji were bewildering.

Baba carried a big bat to defend himself against

hungry wolves. The journey was unforgettable and inspiring. The young boys changed songs about their grapes. The voices touched the heart of deserts. Footsteps of their animals added music to their harmonious lyrics and made it even enjoyable.

The destination was not as pleasant as the journey itself. The King had signed a disgraceful treaty with the British Empire. Kabul still smelled blood. The British Army had slaughtered every soldier they faced. Tyranny governed and cruelty oppressed citizens. When the young grape sealers reached Kabul, they still chanted songs about their grapes and mentioned names of heroes and traitors in their lyrics. They were not afraid of the British Empire.

Hussani is a virtue of beauty,

My son, come and eat grape

Kishmishi is sweet of farmers,

My son, come and eat grape

Wali Mamad is a big villain,

My son, come and eat grape

Ghowla Dan is a bogy of deserts,

My son, come and eat grape

Kandahari is like the hair of beloved

My son, come and eat grape

Mir Bacha is the undefeated hero,

My son, come and eat grape

Sayibi is like honey for young boys,

My son, come and eat grape

My son, come and eat grape

My son, come and eat grape

***

The name of Akbar is everywhere,

My son, come and eat grape

Aminullah is the king of Kings

My son, come and eat the grape,

They are our sons and our blood

My son, come and eat a grape.

Hussani, Kishmishi, Ghowla Dan, and Kandahari were names of grapes. Wali Mamad was a general who betrayed his nation and served the British Empire. Akbar Khan (Wazir Akbar Khan Ghazi), Aminullah (Nayib Aminullah Khan Mujaheed), and Mir Bacha (Mir Bacha Khan) were sons of

Kohdaman who fought against the British Empire.

Baba wore a fur coat. A fur coat lasted for several years. He had a short fur coat, which the edges of his coat reached his thigh. Fur coats were made in Istalif of Afghanistan. The cover of coats was made of sheepskin, while the inside was made of the goat hair. In winters, Baba brought Gul Chehra a bottle of grape sap. People who had a garden in Kohdaman collected barbed plants, and then placed grapes inside them. They pounded and paddled the grapes with their bare feet until they drained everything from grapes. They poured the juice of the grape in a big pan and boiled them until they turned solid. They called it grape sap. In Baba's village (Kalakan), girls prepared the sap differently. They used sticks to drain sap from grapes in a jar made of mud. They called it Moon Sap. Every time Gul Chehra received moon sap from Baba; in return, she gave him green tea and clothes for making a turban.

During summers when the weather was hot and humid; Baba and his friends stayed inside a mosque in Qulai-e-Haji. It was an old mosque and barely a few people visit it. A beautiful dome was built next to the mosque. It was the shrine of Haji Saddu Din. Saddu Din was a poet and a follower of Ansari, the famous poet. The mosque was home for many travelers.

(11)

FRIENDSHIP WITH A DONKEY

A donkey is a poor indiscreet animal,
But he is dear when he carries your bags,

Donkey, a poor, harmless, and friendly animal was a good companion of grape sellers. The poor animal spent long harsh days and nights on hay and grass he found on dried deserts. The vigorous and strong shoes of the men with nails around them did not bear the unbeatable difficult journey, but the plate attached to poor donkeys' feet was strong and could tolerate many more journeys without any trouble. Elders believe that donkeys are friendly and loyal animals, and one must be proud of having them.

"Among us humans, a few those who had a donkey led the nations."

Moses, the barefoot prophet of Israel who drowned Pharaoh in Nile River; Jesus, the victorious prophet, who cured blinds and resurrected dead people; Mohammad, the prophet who gave justice by defending poor people and fighting against oppressors, they all had a donkey.

Horses of world conquerors are forgotten, but the name of a donkey, this barefoot animal is still on everyone's tongue – every day, twelve months and 365 days.

History has not forgotten the donkey of Mullah Nasrudin (mendicant). It is mentioned every day among people in stories, jokes, and tales, but barely, we witness such notable mentions of any other animal in entire human history.

(12)

BABA

Baba had aged. He did not have the strength as he had before. He left everything behind and spent the rest of his life at his garden. He enjoyed spending time with villagers and helping them. He did not travel to Kabul. Besides his garden, he went to the mosque, prayed and returned home. His son had grown up. He was a young, brave and honest man. His friends counted on him and he was famous for his courage, heroism, and intelligence.

Baba gave him the responsibility of traveling to Kabul and selling woods and grapes. Baba hung out his turban on the wall next to his Mashk (bottle). The Mashk reminded him of the battles he endured with his comrades against foreigners' in Kasa Burj. His wish was that when he dies, they must put his Mashk under his head in his grave, so that it may bring him mercy.

(13)

LALA

His son had grown up. He was a strong fearless man. He was born and raised in a small village, but he had the skills of a good leader. He fought against oppressors and villains and defended innocent children, widows, and men. He inspired and led the villagers.

He was a great listener. He knew his people needed him because he always thought about his people. He did not like rich people, because he knew they had robbed his people. Government officials sought a bribe from farmers and traders and when they did not receive it, they made excuses and harassed them. Officials feared him and whenever they encounter him, they let go of the matter for another day. When he was just a boy, his father took him to school, but his rebellious nature put him in trouble.

Once upon a time, an instructor punished his classmate without any reason, he stood up for him. The instructor banned him from attending the school. His parents knew about his untamed nature. When he had no instructor to teach him the way of life, he kneeled to Mother Nature and learned.

He was a gifted person. He quickly grasped the context social, political and economic dilemmas in his country. He learned from every single event that happened around him. He could not read, but he could understand and comprehend. His father tried many times to send him back to school, but he had made his mind.

His father told him stories about their ancestors and the wars they fought. He wanted to ignite a fire of interest in him to read and write, but he knew the whole story. Even though he could not read, but the stories he heard from his father added up to the anger and grudge he already had against the officials. Among all the stories, the story of three patriots who fought against the British Empire bothered him the most. The brave men fought to defend their country and they were brutally murdered.

They were Mohammad Jan Khan Ghazi, Mullah Mashk Aalam, and Mowlana Abdul Ghafoor, the three inspiring leaders and patriots. They were brave and smart, and no one could undermine them. They were the reason why the British army failed in Afghanistan. They defeated the British army, but later they were betrayed and brutally murdered. The story of their death was a tragedy for the nation. Lala was inspired by the story and he asked his father to describe them.

It was a dreadful and gloomy night. Black clouds covered the sky of Kabul. The three heroes were invited to the palace of the king for a dinner. They came alone because they believed the palace of the king is like their home. These men had convinced people to end the war once they defeated the enemy. Everyone had agreed to accept the king as their leader. Dinner ended well with a smile on everyone's face. The three brave men left the palace and headed towards their homes.

It was midnight when a mob of equestrians ambushed them from all sides. It was an order given by the king. The soldiers sieged and arrested them. The ingrate army of the king chained hands and feet of the men and covered their mouth and eyes with black cloths. The King and his masters had already outnumbered people in the city by bringing more soldiers and heavy British weaponry. Once the King felt protected, he gave the order to take the three heroes to the north.

The King's army repeatedly moved the men from one place to another. They were hungry, thirsty and tired. They were starving. They could not see or say anything. Their hands almost melted from exacerbating pain. They were firmly shackled with chains. They were not allowed to sleep or pray for their soul.

It was treachery plotted by the king, his friends and advisors. The guards did not know the men. The desert of Aab Do Kotal (River between two valleys) 15 miles far from Mazar-e-Sharif, was a slaughterhouse chosen for the Patriots.

Traitors who lead the king's army were obsessed with killing Patriots. They could not wait for a minute. They were like hyenas circling a prey. They had made gibbets for the Patriots on a dark desert. Everyone thought the king have captured traitors, and he is going to hang them in the desert. No one knew the king and his men were about to hang the three patriots. People loved these men and wanted to serve under their leadership.

It was dawn and the aroma of spring scented the desert. Tulips colored the desert. It was enticing picturesque. The chirping of birds awakened everyone. The three blindfolded heroes with shackles on their hands and feet were sent to gallows. Their skin dried and their throat parched.

They were hanged to death and buried without any respect.

(14)

TWO COMMANDERS

Baba often mentioned the name of Wazir Akbar Khan whenever he talked to his son about bravery. He knew how to make it an emotional story. Wazir was a prisoner, and he freed himself from Bukhara Prison and joined rebels to fight against the enemy. Wazir met fighters from Panjsher, Gulbahar, Kohistan, and Charikar then headed towards the capital, Kabul. Baba told his son that his grandpa and other men accompanied Wazir in that historical battle.

Legends say that Wazir's mother sent him a letter and left a couple of her hair strings inside the letter and told him "This is your mother hair, and the enemy controls it. This is your dignity and pride being hurled by the enemy and foreigners, if you do not come soon and rescue us, you are not my son. I curse you."

Wazir and his men entered Kabul; they spent the night in Kalakan and prepared the army for the decisive war. Wazir knew how to inspire his men; he fought in the frontline and had no fear. It was a bloody war. Wazir was badly wounded and he could not move. He asked his men to carry his body to Mazar-e-Sharif a city in the north of Afghanistan and bury him there. He told his men that when I am alive, no one can disrespect me, but when I am dead, I don't want the enemy to disrespect me. That night Wazir died and his men carried his body on their shoulders to Kalakan and then Mazar-e-Sharif.

Baba always talked about Sardar Mohammad Ayub Khan. Sardar was a champion of Maiwand Battle; the second Anglo-Afghan war. Afghans defeated Great Britain and killed more than one thousand enemy soldiers. Baba told his son, Wazir Akbar Khan and Mohammad Ayub Khan were real commanders and leaders. They loved their people and country. They never betrayed their people. They fought and died with honor and dignity. They are a symbol of courage and heroism.

(15)

GRUDGES

Baba wanted his son to have a perfect picture of his country. He walked with him and told him about abandoned and empty forts in villages. He showed him forts of Mir Bacha Khan, and Imam Sahib Ghulam Jan, and another uninhabited fort in Deh Qazi. He also took him to see the fort of Tutmadra and Dubali. Lala had also visited many other forts in Kabul and neighboring provinces. The forts belonged to Jalandhar Khan and Abdul Karim Khan. His father told him that people who owned these forts were patriotic leaders and commanders. They were a symbol of unity and peace in the country. When the puppet government came in power, most of them were either killed or they fled to India.

Baba told his son that forts were used for gatherings like a council. The puppet government sieged the villages and attacked on the forts. The men fought an unwinnable war and lost it. The government turned the forts into human slaughterhouses. Now, everyone is afraid of walking closer to the forts, because it is haunted.

Baba also told his son about the Kasa Burj battle. The story was tragic and Lala got emotional and trembled. Lala stood up, kissed his father turban and Mashk. The story contained painful and heartbreaking layers. Corruption, embezzlement of public property, injustice, torture of innocents, oppression; all these made Lala angry and added to his resentments against tyrants.

Lala helped his father in their garden. Whenever he finished the work, he met his friends in the mosque and discussed with them the fate of his people and country. Summers were different; they sat under a tree and talked for hours. They exchanged stories and ideas.

Stories from Kabul were the most interesting. They eagerly waited for people to bring news and stories from the capital. Lala knew how important it was for them to know what was happening in Kabul. Every story thought him a lesson. He was a very detailed oriented person. If a storyteller left something complicated, he asked him questions until the story was free of ambiguity. The stories were painful and often the audience hated the storyteller for adding to their pains. Lala listened to every single story and wanted to know what his people were going through. He wanted to share the pain and find a way to help them one day.

His friends knew that Lala memorized all the sad stories with details, but barely remembered good stories. Lala was a focal point and whenever new audience came in, he told them the stories. He knew that sad stories could unite his people and make them strong against the enemy. The stories were simple; the real-life story of people under a tyrant and puppet government. Lala wanted to kindle the souls and gave them strengths.

(16)

DUNG

Once upon a time during cold and harsh winter, two little girls were fighting on the streets of Kabul. They hurt and scratched each other's face by snatching hair and dipping their nails in each other's skin. Kabul was like an icebox. As the fight continued, drops of blood glaciated on their innocent cheek. Both girls had a saddlebag for collecting animal dung. They had to collect and bring dung for the night to not freeze from cold. They also used the dung to make fire and cook dinner on them. The two nascent girls fought like gladiators. In the darkest and dreadful days of Kabul, they were one of the many ill-fated souls bothered by poverty.

It was a battle of two hungry creatures; a battle between two innocent pigeons; two barefoot little girls in the freezing days of a brutal winter.

They fought over animal dung; dirty dung that had no value and worth anywhere in the world. Yet, on that freezing cold and stormy day, for those two little poor girls, it meant everything. As they fought and hurt each other for dung, sounds of an elite horse with a fat man on it rambled. The man had big twisted mustaches, an elegant tuque made from lambskin on his head and a sericeous black coat. The combination added to his solemnity making him a monarch. Black smoke from his pipe formed circles in the air and his black classy glasses petrified him than he seemed. When the horseman left, the girls made peace.

Lala asked the storyteller: The horseman gave them something? The storyteller continued. No, the two girls were fighting over dung. The kindhearted horse dropped another one. They both had something to take home. There was no need to fight.

(17)

A LIVER

Once upon a time, a man was walking along the butcheries in Shahi Bazar of Kabul. He bought a book and he was returning home. It was evening and the sun headed behind the mountains. On the other side of the street, he saw a pale and weak sculpture leaned on the wall. It grabbed his attention and he walked toward it. As he got closer, he saw the object moved like a zombie. It was an old poor skinny man with dirty and torn clothes. He was talking to a butcher.

The butcher said, "I am closing the shop after five minutes; the day is over."

The poor man appealed" I want a sheep liver for my son. I only want half of a liver for my son who recovered today from sickness after a month of struggle. The doctor told us, we must give him sheep liver to gain strength and fight the diseases. His mother and I have put everything together to buy half a liver for him. That is all we have please".

The angry butcher responded, "I do not have any liver."

The man pointed to livers hanging on chains" I see five fresh livers out there."

The butcher retorted "The livers are for the minister's dogs."

The old man was disappointed and wiped his tears and walked away.

He went to the butcher, begged and asked him to sell half of a liver for the old man, but the stonehearted butcher did not listen to him either.

(18)

A SUICIDE

People had gathered in front of a wealthy merchant's house in Shoor Bazaar. The market was a crowded place and most often it was filled with strangers traveling from far districts. The crowds were trying to circle the house located next to the market like sheep. Police officers in red uniforms and shiny whistles on their hand pushed away from the crowd. It seemed a teenager had committed suicide in an underground hall. Eyes and ears were eager to know everything. After almost two hours, a wealthy merchant with Kashmiri Shawl and shiny deluxe shoes, and a curly black beard and big mustache, walked out of the house.

The police officers stood in line and respected him like they were his soldiers. The rich merchant had already concurred with officers. The wealthy man commanded.

"Remove his body from my house, and give it to his family and relatives if he has any. He must not be buried in our cemetery. He has committed suicide. He is a disgrace."

The officers brought the dead body on an old carpet and left it on the street. The crowd started mumbling.

A man said: He has hanged himself up.

A man standing closer to the dead body said: He has been murdered, his pale face looks like a martyred.

Another stranger said: What a handsome boy. He looks still alive and speaks to you. His striking eyes are open, his clothes are torn and he is barefoot.

The discussions, dialogues, and whispers burst and silenced with a sympathetic and screaming voice of a woman among the crowd.

"Oh, my precious young son, my poor son," Why you did not listen to me, why you did not have mercy for me, you made me miserable."

The curious crowd learned she is the mother of the unknown person. Everyone was shocked. Mother is precious and sacred and everyone felt the pain the poor mother was going through.

The grieving mother with a devastated voice continued.

"My son was a gardener for this merchant. Two years ago, my son got engaged with a girl in our neighborhood. They loved each other wholeheartedly. For the engagement ceremony, we borrowed some money from this merchant with a very high-interest rate. My son worked hard and did everything to pay his debts on time, but he could not do it. The interest rate increased as every day passed and my son drowned under debt. We had a small garden. We had inherited it from our parents, and we farmed on it for our livelihood. The merchant seized our garden, and it was not enough for him, so he forced my son to work for him for two years without any payments. A few days ago, my son's father-in-law asked us to provide money for the wedding ceremony. He had warned us that they had to leave this neighborhood due to unemployment and they will take their daughter with them. My son asked the merchant to borrow him money for the wedding and he will work for him forever. The stonehearted wealthy merchant did not help him. My son was lost and disappointed, and now he is dead. I am not sure if he committed suicide or he was killed. For the sake of God, someone please help us. This greedy bastard killed my son." She grabbed the merchant's door chain with both hands.

The police officers pushed away from the poor women and made her leave the area. The officers put the dead body on the back of a donkey and sent him with his mother towards a ceremony. Since then, no one ever heard what happened to that ill-fated old lady.

Lala was hurt with these painful stories and it ignited a fire inside him. The stories were like pieces of brick building up like an empire against tyranny and oppression. No one ever knew who will destroy the foundation of tyranny and oppression on this great land. Would it be a scholar who reads and writes under the lights of a candle and smells smoke every night? Would it be an army general who had oppressed his own people with his sword? Would it be a prince, who lurk, stalk and ambush on the public properly and seized them? Would it be a greedy wealthy merchant who worships money? Or would it be a force rising from ashes and among the oppressed masses?

It would be an illiterate man; a man who only has an old coat and sells grapes for a living. He does not belong to any wealthy or elite family. He even cannot read and write. He is brave and he fights for justice. Everything he sees and hears adds to his maturity. It is not easy for him to bear all the pains.

They bother him a lot.

Corruption, ethnic cleansing, systematic discrimination, robbery and harassment by authorities for centuries had paved a way for a great revolution. Abuse of power by greedy wealthy elites, seizing properties by tyrants, disrespecting people's tradition and culture, belittling people's dignity and pride further had added to their hatred against them.

Lala's bravery, decency, and fearlessness had inspired youths and they joined him in his journey. They all gathered around him after work and practiced combat. The contests were wrestling, throwing stones, fighting with a stick, jumping and running. Anyone who could fight with a stick and a knife were prepared to fight with a sword. Their contests attracted villagers and they watched them as they practiced.

Leadership, physical strength, and bravery gave Lala the responsibility of managing his team. Everyone followed and listened to him. Lala's name became a symbol of motivation in Kohdaman.

Days after days more youth from other villages joined Lala. It was not easy to join his team. One had to show bravery and courage first and must be physically strong. After so many races and contests, only twelve young men passed psychological and physical tests and joined the band of brothers.

In the outskirt of the lonely mountains, the men gathered at the shrine of Khoja Sabs Posh and signed a pack of friendship. They promised to be honest, loyal and defend their belief, culture, and people against enemy and oppressors. They had two things in common. First, they hated corrupt officials, who committed all forms of violence; and second, the greedy stonehearted wealthy merchants who drained the entire nation.

Lala's real name was Habibullah, but everyone called him Lala. Only one person among the twelve members could read and write. Whenever they needed to know about a past event, the literate member read them a history book. The bond of brothers became a school of thought. The principals were very simple; unity, honesty, and devotion. They woke up early mornings, helped their neighbors, fought for the rights of poor people and stood against wealthy tyrants.

They did not fear government officials. They robbed greedy oppressors as the Robin Hood did. Their soul and heart were ready for a battle. They could stay hungry and thirsty for days. Nothing could stop them. It was a tough struggle for them and they were ready for it.

A man's soul rests in his heart, and those who have

a soul inside their heart will never give up. They put a tent under trees of Khawaja Sabs Posh shrine. They conducted their meetings inside the tent. The only thing that could stop them was the slaughterhouse of King. The bond of brothers had a strong foundation, but still naïve to public eyes.

The struggle started from a small village in Kalakan. His village had turned into a safe haven for them. Authorities no more could harass the public. The brothers went after robbers and thugs and punished them. They always defeated the enemy and seized their guns and ammunition. Lala hated corrupt officials, robbers, and bullies. He stood against them. He saw muggers and officials in the same clothes. They both seized people's properties. Most nights Lala could not fall asleep thinking about his people.

The bond of brothers defended orphans and widows against crook officials and never allowed them to harass anyone. Lala had grown up into a strong young man. He was a headache for criminals and dictators. People loved him for his bravery and courage. Tyrants finally found a way to oppress the bond of brothers and made sure Lala and his friends could no more help his people and seek justice for victims.

(19)

THE TALE OF BUKHARA

His parents and relatives wanted him to stay away from his friends. They feared that his friends may defame his personality. Things were getting out of control. The brothers challenged the government authority and his parents fear that officials will entrap him. The tyrant government labeled individuals with whom they interact, and when they did not like something, they use national force to suppress it. His parents feared that Lala could get in trouble due to his friends.

He did not give up on his friends. He worked as a gardener in Hussain Kot village. The garden belonged to a man called Mustofiul Mamalik. His friends came and joined him. His father asked him to marry the daughter of a farmer from Hussain Kot village. It was an arranged marriage. Lala spent three years in Hussain Kot village.

His parents thought giving him a family, responsibility for a wife and children would give him peace of mind, but he was an ambitious leader. When Amanullah Khan became King, the government seized the gardens and Lala returned home to his village, Kalakan. Lala often visited his in-laws in Hussain Kot Village. The King bestowed the gardens to King of Bukhara.

King of Bukhara had fled to Afghanistan. The Red Army had invaded his country and his life had become miserable. Lala hated Russians. The Red Army had brutally murdered innocent children, women, and men. They also had slaughtered Afghan soldiers dispatched in support of Bukhara's King. The stories hurt him. Lala wanted to know what really happened in Bukhara.

"Why people of Bukhara could not defend their country. How the King and his family are alive while his country bleeds? How the Red Army slaughtered thousands of nascent Afghan soldiers in Bukhara, but people of Bukhara did not fight?"

Russians had committed atrocious. They killed innocent people, burned homes, invaded people's dignity and honor. Lala didn't know why people of Bukhara give up their freedom so easily.

Amir Sayed Aalam Khan, the exiled king of Bukhara attended his horses on Fridays in a desert. He had brought horses from Bukhara. The king watched his handsome slaves wrestle and sword fight. Lala watched the contests and wanted to compete against the King's men. Lala watched the games on three consecutive Fridays. Lala asked if he could attend the races, and the King of Bukhara allowed him to compete against his men.

Lala saw men trying to tame a horse. The King was bothered by the event. No one could control the horse. Lala asked for permission to tame the horse and he was granted his wish. Lala knew nothing about horses, but he was physically strong and brave. He put a struggle and tamed the horse. Later, he attended sword fighting contents and won the competition. The King was surprised.

The King asked him to come and work for him. Lala refused his offer. He told the King, that he has old parents and he needs to take care of them. He also suggested, if he decided to go back to his country and fight the Russians, he would join him.

Lala's words touched the King. He asked his clerk to note his name and address. Lala never thought the day would come for the King to go back to his country and send for him to join him.

(20)

A GRAPE SELLER

Lala sold grapes in summers and firewood in winters. Everyone had to do something to feed their family. His untamed nature did not want to spend his valuable life like a regular person. He wanted to change the fate of his people. He was a noble person and he listened to his father. His friends loved him and they wanted to spend time with Lala. When he became a grape seller, his friends also became grape sellers. When he became a firewood seller, his friends also became firewood sellers. Lala and his friends traveled from their village in Kalakan to Kabul to sell grapes and firewood. The journey was long and they carried the products on the back of their donkeys. They used donkeys because donkeys are strong animals. They are slow, but they can travel for miles without any trouble.

Winters were harsh and cold and they only traveled twice per week. However, summers were exciting and they made several trips in just a single week. They started their journey at night because the sky was beautiful and stars shined.

Every time he left home, Lala kissed his parents' hands to pay respect and get their blessings. He put baskets of grapes on his donkey and headed towards Kabul with his friends. His gave him a special basket of handpicked grapes. The grapes were for Gul Chehra, the god-sister of Lala's father. He delivered the grapes to Gul Chehra at Palace of Princess. His father was sick and could not travel anymore. He listened to his father and delivered his message and gifts.

It was not safe to travel. The roads were in chaos. He had a pleasant smile on his face every time he returned home. His father had given him his knife and asked him to keep it with him at all times. The rural boys traveled like a caravan of kings and emperors. Lala assigned everyone a responsibility. They sang songs and their voices echoed in the mountains.

Most often Lala and his friends arrived in Kabul at dawn. The city was lonely and everyone asleep. Lala and his friends put down baskets of grapes on the ground and let the donkeys sleep. They sat next to their animals. He was tired and his feet hurt, but still, he could not sleep. In addition to selling grapes, he has another responsibility. He had to deliver a special basket of grapes to Gul Chehra. He had not gone to the Palace and it was difficult to find it. When he arrived at the palace, he felt the pain of the residents. The town was in pain due to civil, tribal and familial conflicts.

Wars between princes and kings had destroyed Kabul. Wars between Abdul Rahman Khan and Sardar Mohammad Ishaq had brought tragedy. Wars between Mohammad Ayub Khan and Abdul Rahman Khan had sent the country centuries back. These disastrous wars cost the lives of thousands of innocent people and the destruction of the country. The tribal and civil wars had helped the neighboring countries to interfere in Afghanistan's affairs. Most parts of the country were occupied by foreigners.

Sadly! Our nation suffered severely and lives were lost for nothing. Whenever a new Amir or King took power, he destroyed whatever his predecessors had built to discredit and remove his name from history. It happened for centuries. We lost our civilization and became a ruined land.

Shirpoor was no more a Palace for Kings. The new resident for the king was the ARG. Gul Chehra had aged and lost her eyesight. She had no hope of returning to her parents or her homeland, Bamyan. She knew that either her parents were dead, or they believed Gul Chehra was dead.

Gul Chehra spent her entire life within the walls of a castle like a prisoner. She knew how violent kings and their men could become. She listened to innocent men, women, and children being tortured by Kings and his men. Humans were treated like pets. She always wanted to help innocent children and women, but she could not do it and it hurt her more than anything else.

She wanted to tell his brother what happened to her. It was her last hope to share her story with someone she could trust. She wanted him to send a message to her parents in Bamyan and check if they were still alive. Every week, she waited to see Baba, but instead, his son came to visit her. She was happy seeing her nephew, but she missed her brother. Gul Chehra treated Lala like a son and gave him green tea and clothes for his brother.

She knew her brother was sick. She concluded that she might never see him again and had to share her story with Lala. The story of her life cut Lala's heart into pieces. He wanted to seek revenge, but Gul Chehra calmed him down. Gul Chehra told him that the Queen had been nice to her. She told him that the poor queen had lost her authority. Her means of survival depended on income from gardens she inherited from her parents. The Queen had two young daughters and Gul Chehra look after them. Kings family members and relatives were entitled to monthly stipends from the national treasury. When Amanullah Khan became the king, he cut the monthly stipend for the king's family.

(21)

ALMOND BLOSSOM

On those old days, every kingdom had a harem. The harem was a special place, where they kept the women far away from strangers. The guardians of the king's harem were very strict on Hijab. Whenever the queen's ride arrived in the city, the guards walked ahead of the ride, blocked the roads and hit people with a stick to close their eyes.

Get blind! Get blind!

People turned around and closed their eyes. King's family and relatives were kept away from the public's eye. This tradition was enforced by the king's guardians. However, if you did not belong to the royal family, they would not care if you covered yourself or not. Poor women worked like slaves. They were deprived of their basic rights. The king's guardians did not care and value anyone other than the royal family.

Guardians of the king's court respected Gul Chehra as they respected their grandma. Strangers were not allowed to enter the palace, however; when Lala arrived at the palace, Gul Chehra made sure he was permitted to get in. Guardians observed his behavior and after a while learning that he was a nobleman and never made eye contact with any women in the palace.

Lala asked his friends to look after his donkey. He headed towards the palace to meet Gul Chehra. He had a jar of jam and some other dried fruit. The city was covered with snow. Sun barely melted snows at some parts of the city. It was cold and felt like spring was on the way.

The almond trees had barely blossomed. Cactus and flowers scarcely showed their face. A bevy of quails and horde of geese flew over Kabul city. The blue-eyed sky looked at Kabul through the shallow clouds. Immigrant ducks traveled from the south to the north. They wanted to cross the Hindu Kush Mountains and arrive at their destination before dawn. Chirping of birds, and singing of nightingales was mesmerizing.

Lala finished his prayer in Pul Kheshti Mosque and returned to the Queen's Palace to bid farewell with Gul Chehra. He tightened his turban around his waist to leave the Palace when Gul Chehra called him.

"Son! Please cut a branch from that almond three and give it to the lady waiting under the tree."

A young beautiful girl stood under the tree. She was trying to cut a branch, but she could hardly touch the leaves. Lala without making an eye contact walked around and climbed the tree. He cut a thick branch and gave it to the stranger. She blushed out of shy and walked away. She climbed the stairs and disappeared. Her silky blue dress and lazuli scarf added to her beauty. The simplicity of her appearance, purity of her looks and civility of her manners ignited a fire in Lala's heart. It was like a moment when a hunter throws an arrow in the air without aiming and it accidentally hits an innocent bird in the wing and wounds it.

On his way back home, the sun had generously melted the snow. Flowers and plants smiled back at the sun. Spring was everywhere. Deserts were lonely and abandoned, but they had the company of travelers. Donkeys were the allies creating a rhythm to the sound of nature by their hanging bells on their chests. Nothing had changed; except Lala who felt differently.

He did not know what had happened to him. The earth, and sky; the sun and air they all felt different.

Everywhere he looked, he saw that innocent face and the almond tree. He faced the same phantasm every single day. The face appeared everywhere; in abandoned deserts, in white smoky snows, in the crystalline sky, in the reflex of the sea, in the smile of sunshine, in the blow of wind, even in his own image. He attended meetings and listened to his friends, but his heart was somewhere else. Lala and his friends stopped at the sanctum of Ansari, a famous Persian poet for a couple of hours to rest. Everyone started praying, but Lala's dreams and wishes were different than before. He did not know what he wanted anymore. What his heart wanted from him was too much destruction for his struggle to freedom and it wounded him.

(22)

LOVE AND MADNESS OR BOTH?

The assassination of Habibullah Khan, Amir of Afghanistan who was shot in the head in Kala Gush district of Laghman province by a known person whose identity raises many questions and the historians even avoid crediting him the murder laid a path for his third son Amanullah Khan to sit in the throne.

During Amanullah's reign, Afghanistan gained its independence from Great Britain. Independence was heavy and cost many lives. People enjoyed freedom for the first time in a while. Slavery and servitude were abolished. Prisoners were freed from disgraceful oppression. Gul Chehra was gone. Her dreams of freedom for slaves had died with her too. She dreamed of visiting her homeland, Bamyan. Lala and his friends still sold grapes and firewood.

Public schools were founded in cities and districts. During the reign of Amir Habibullah Khan, only two formal schools; Habibia School and military school existed. With Amanullah in power, new organizations replaced old ones. Heavy taxation system which was based on primary goods such as wheat, Ghee, and rice was replaced by cash. Government departments were established and the national flag from rich officials' doors was brought down.

People had hope about their future and believed new vital foundations will be established for their better future. Discrimination, bribery, corruption, and nepotism will go away. Monthly stipend which was given to every Mohammadzai individuals (Pashtun ethnic leaders) as a privilege will be stopped. People will not be hanged without trial and court decisions. Innocent people will not be aimed and shot by cannons. Dark wells which poor people were sent to rotten will be destroyed and no more nightmares will be gifted to innocent people. Suspects will not be punished by throwing them off the mountain cliff. No more women's hair will be tied to a horse's tail as a form of domestic punishment.

People hoped that all these reforms will happen within the framework of law and independence. Whatever the outcomes are, people never expected that the reforms will question their traditions and beliefs. The traditions and beliefs had become a foundation for every single person.

For the last thirteen hundred years, they believed in those values and it had given them hope and prosperity. They were the groundwork for coming to this world and leaving this world peacefully. Violating any of those values was considered being against the will of God. They fought for independence and this violation would have also countered the independence they achieved by giving their lives for it.

Unfortunately, the uneducated bodies in government offices did not understand that bringing fundamental reforms and expanding western values in Afghanistan in such a crucial time was a dangerous step towards destruction. They did not know that every single individual was ready to stand against any violation and fight. They should have known that before planting a seed ground must be ready.

Religious scholars felt that reforms were against the will of people and their belief, and they doubted that these changes will bring more darkness than prosperity to people. Government authorities who were appointed based on favoritism did not know what the public wanted for the country. Authorities had forgotten the sacrifices and believed people owned them.

Unfortunately, at such a crucial time, due to hasty reforms, education the most important need of the nation was sacrificed. Schools and educators still believed that teaching subjects like geography at school were a waste of time.

Government authorities didn't know that mosques were the prime educational center for every child. They didn't know that people were keen to learn and listen to what is told in a mosque rather than in a school. They didn't know that battles of churches and schools had happened in many countries, and blood were shed because of their separation.

Authorities were unable to reason and provide better motives; however, they were engaged in bribery and corruption. The exploitation fueled a fire and day by day people felt pessimist about reforms and changes. Conflicts ignited at some parts of the country. The government used military forces to push back. The distance between people and government widened.

(23)

A FOREIGN POLICY

Major changes took place in Afghanistan's foreign policy. The young government established and strengthened its relationship with the USSR (Union of Soviet Socialist Republics). The heart-melting manipulative compliments of the USSR touched heart the young government. They blindly believed that Russia is the only supporter of the nation. Russians had never helped the Afghan government when Afghans were fighting for Independence against Great Britain. However, authorities within the new establishment considered Russia a true supporter of Independence. It was obvious that Russia always looked for an opportunity to find Afghanistan engulfed in the civil war so they could get closer to the warm waters of Afghanistan.

Russians often cowardly attacked and took parts of sovereign states.

The partition of Panjawa, a significant part of Afghanistan was occupied during that period of the time by Russians. Invasion on Bukhara also happened at the time when Afghanistan was in a battle with Great Britain. When Afghans won the battle, the Russians did not recognize Afghanistan's independence. Russia recognized Afghanistan only when most of the countries had already recognized Afghanistan as an independent country, including Great Britain. It seemed more like a turkey after the thanks-giving.

Afghanistan's Ministry of Foreign Affairs was behind all the plots. The USSR and the Minister strategized to extend and strengthen Afghanistan's relationship with the USSR. All communications, minutes and documents were hidden at the Ministry of Foreign Affairs, and away from public eyes. Afghanistan did not benefit being an ally of USSR. People of Afghanistan did not like Russians at all and they had a sense of hatred against them. They had forcefully taken Panjawa, a beautiful part of Afghanistan. Russians had a history of attacking small Muslim nations in Central Asian. They had coerced and forced indigenous people to leave their homeland and migrate across the Amu River to Afghanistan. They had occupied one after another.

Bukhara, Samarqand, Farghana, Khiwa, and Khowarzm were already occupied by Russians. The oppression and cruelty of Russians against indigenous people of central Asia boiled the blood of every individual. They had a scar in their heart that would never go away. Russians were against the independence of small nascent nations. There were so many reasons for the young government to avoid strengthening relations with the Russians, but the government ignored the voices of millions.

People felt the government is lost. Maybe, they were bewitched by the false promises and had forgotten their duty to support their brothers across the border. People asked religious leaders to prioritize their needs. Afghanistan must support vulnerable people of Central Asian states. The scholars who worked for the government knew that a mistake was being committed. They knew the consequences of ignoring the nation's will, but they kept quiet and looked for irrelevant excuses somewhere else.

Afghans welcomed and embraced migrants. They showed them love and brotherhood and made them feel home. Often, historians do not write about the generosity of Afghans. The government went further and declared that any opposition to friendship with Russians will be an opposition to the independence of Afghanistan and the punishment will be death. Afghan government believed that the only ally and friend of Afghanistan is Russia, and the only enemy is Great Britain.

Influential Muslim leaders who fled the occupied lands and migrated to Afghanistan met the king and tried to reason with him, but the government was blind by the false promises. Anwar Baig, General Rashid, and Mashhoor Usmani traveled to Dushanbe, the capital of Tajikistan, gathered an army and fought the USSR occupation. More men from Afghanistan fled to Tajikistan to fight USSR's occupation. General Usmani led the army against the Russians. Mowlawi Abdu Hai, an influential leader from Panjshir of Afghanistan joined General Usmani. Abdul Hai had already lost his father in a resistance battle against Russians' occupation. General Usmani named Abdul Hai, Shaikhulah, a title that is earned through dedication and sacrifice for a good cause. When Abdul Hai and other leaders joined General Usmani's army, a national uprising ignited in Afghanistan and its smoke even reached India.

The Afghan government-appointed Mohammad Nadir Khan as his special envoy and commander to the Northern provinces to stop people from joining Anwar Baig, but it was found later that Mohammad Nadir Khan was assisting Anwar Baig rather than stopping him. The government felt things were getting out of control. Nadir Khan was fired from his position and was appointed as ambassador to Paris. When Abdul Hai returned to Afghanistan from Tajikistan, he was imprisoned in Khan Abad Prison.

Lala was prepared for such a day. He traveled to Tajikistan with his friends and joined Anwar Baig's army. He showed excellence and bravery in battles and caught eyes of generals. Anwar Baig promoted him as an officer and gave him a recommendation letter. That letter of recommendation helped him joined the special division later in Kabul.

When the USSR became aware of Anwar Baig's intentions and danger of his army expansion in Central Asia, they cowardly killed him in Qurghan Tipa during the Eid Days. Horsemen in Muslim traditional clothes approached him and gave his army an impression that they have come to join him, instead they fired at him killing the general and his friends. Death of Anwar Baig created a distance between government and people and upset religious leaders.

Inexperienced and immature authorities stuck to government posts like an octopus. They ignored the seriousness of the issue. People expressed their frustration and hatred, but the King was given a different story. The security situation got worse.

Highways got closed. Robbers befriended corrupt officials, and in many cities, the government and robbers joined forces. A competition for the accumulation of wealth started between governors. Government lost absolute control over the public. No one obeyed laws and listened to government authorities. The government sent religious messages to make people embrace his orders, but people know the hypocrisy. Government policies and orders became meaningless.

The government-sponsored and conducted a campaign of no Hijab for women. In villages, women only wore a scarf while their feet and hands were uncovered to perform farming and animal husbandry chorus, while in cities women were fully covered, including their hands, face, and feet since they had no productive duties. The campaign angered rural people and they took it very seriously. People saw it as a spot on their dignity, pride, national heritage, and religious belief. The situation got out of control and the King was being misinformed about the affairs. The king traveled to Europe. The King's family including the queen appeared in a western dress in Europe and it added to the frustration back in the country. In the absence of the King, authorities increased taxes and decided to collect them as soon as possible before the arrival of the King. North of Kabul, from Kohdaman to

Bamyan and Taghab, this region became a center of disobedience against the government. In the West, the Herat province started the same uprising.

The authorities had plotted to:

- To ignore tax receipts and collect tax from the public without verifying the documents.
- Those who did not have cash, the authorities seized their businesses, properties, gardens, and houses.
- The values of the properties were set by the authorities very low when seizing them in return for tax.
- Those who did not have property were jailed and put to hard labor.

People in the north of Kabul were highly suppressed by the authorities. They were the poorest of all and the most vulnerable to the orders. Authorities used military forces to collect money from people and conveyed the order in a brutal manner. People in Herat province were better off and they could afford it. In the north of Kabul, People got tired of authorities and suddenly they stood against them. King Amanullah Khan who loved his country and wanted to make sure it develops, returned from Europe. The comparison of a luxurious lifestyle in the West and the poor conditions of living in Afghanistan angered him. People hoped that by his return, the violence and oppression will end, especially in the north of Kabul, who had suffered severely under the hammer of authorities. When the King returned, unlike the expectations, he forced changes in people's personal life. The King ordered his people to wear western clothes and leave behind traditional costumes. Turban was replaced by the hat. Asalam Walikom which was a form of religious and traditional greeting was omitted from conversations, instead of taking off the hat and bowing which looked like a joke become common.

Farmers who traveled from villages to Kabul to sell grapes and firewood ornamented their shoes with nails and chains. Jeans and hat become fashion. Most of the hats people wore were left behind from the British army. Those hats were a symbol of victory against invaders, especially Great Britain. Previously, hats were kept in farmhouses, but now shopkeepers, salon workers, massagers, everyone had to follow ridiculous order and wore them. If anyone was found not wearing a hat, authorities fine them.

Friday was replaced with Thursday. Friday was a traditional and religious day for Muslims. They prayed and greet friends and relatives on Friday. Friday was a holiday, but in return Thursday became a holiday. Lunar and Solar calendars were replaced to Gregorian calendar. The flag of Afghanistan changed from Allah Akbar (God is great) to Rostrum and Altar with arts of a mountain and sun.

Islamic scholars who were a student in Deoband Madrassa were given the order to return home, and do not teach at Madrassas or lead the prayers. The last council which was conveyed in Paghman of Kabul showed how people are expressing their dislikes with government approaches, but the authorities mostly agreed with the orders because they felt threatened to agree. When the leaders returned home, gossips started.

Economic development, improvement in the education sector, the establishment of a national council, founding the constitution and other significant changes and reforms were shadowed because of the religious campaigns and addresses. Authorities were very harsh on people of Kohdaman. They faced systematic discrimination. The government even forced them to remove their gardens' walls making their farms vulnerable. Authorities presumed that this would attract foreign tourists. However, biased foreign policy could not provide a room for foreign tourists to visit the country. Forcing one-sided policy on the public without any benefit to their livestock increased people's frustrations. Internal migration reached its climax. Officials ignored the public's frustration and pain resulting in a national bloody uprising. The rivals had dethroned the king and put in power an illiterate grape seller who lived among people and felt their pain.

Great Britain was humiliated due to their defeat in Afghanistan. They always looked for a reason to start a civil war in Afghanistan. India was their colony and they wanted to take back Afghanistan. Britain also feared that Afghanistan was getting closer to the USSR and they did not like it. Afghans hated Great Britain as much as they did the USSR. They kicked them out of their country. At the same time, the USSR invaded Muslim nations in the Central Asian States; they even forcefully had seized Panjway. A mindful citizen can easily know who was responsible for all the chaos and conflicts. Those who credited Great Britain with the national uprising against the Amani Kingdom ignore the pain and suffering of people, and dishonor the heroic acts of leaders who stood against injustice.

(24)

AN ILLITERATE ARMY

Afghanistan faced fundamental changes. Some changes were good while some were destructive. One of the significant positive changes was the improvement of the national army and the establishment of a military division. A Turkish officer who worked for King Amanullah Khan asked the king to establish a military division. Turks were very famous for their military knowledge and tactics. They were victorious in battles. The Ottoman dynasty ruled Turkey. Turkey's relation with the Afghan government was very friendly. Mahmood Tarzi, Afghanistan minister of foreign affairs and a well-known politician had a keen interest in building a relationship with Turkey. During King Habibullah Khan's reign, the people of

Afghanistan sent money and gifts to support the Ottoman Empire in World War II. Founding a new army and improving the quality of the military was something both countries agreed and emphasized on it. Military academy known as Division was a small branch of that initiative. All recruits for the division were voluntary. It was part of the government campaign to train a new generation of soldiers.

Baba was afraid that his son would get in trouble. Authorities in Kalakan village always looked for an excuse to trap Lala and his friends. Fear was real because Lala and his friends stood up against injustice and corruption. Baba also dreamed that one day his son may serve in the Afghan government as an officer. He wanted his son to have peace in his heart and serve under the auspicious flag of his homeland.

Baba asked his son to join government forces and fight enemies. The Davison only focused on practical skills. There was no need for literacy or theatrical studies. Lala and two of his friends who had joined Anwar Baig's army to fight USSR returned to Kabul and upon submission of Anwar Baig's recommendation letter, Lala was admitted to the division. Turkish recruiter also noticed that Lala had a well-suited physical strength, and showed bravery and courage. The untamed rebellious soul of a barefoot grape seller finally had peace serving under the flag of his beloved country.

Lala successfully completed all physical and practical military training. He showed excellence and superiority. Previously, he had attended military training in Tajikistan and fought at frontlines; his previous experience added value to his training at the Division.

When Lala was in Division, nomads of southern parts of Afghanistan under the leadership of Mullah Abdullah (Mullah Lang) and Abdul Karim started a riot against the government. Abdul Karim was the King's relative; both leaders were angered because of religious issues. People thought it was a political coup for power, rather than an uprising for justice.

Lala was sent with many other officers to counter the riot. The soldiers defeated the riot and returned Kabul. Mullah Abdullah was captured, and Abdul Karim had escaped. Lala received a medal of honor for his service and was promoted in the Division. He became famous among his fellow comrades.

To fight criminals, the government recruited an informant from criminal groups to snitch on them. The strategy failed because the informant became a deal breaker between authorities and criminals.

It was almost Eidi-Qurban and people were preparing for the festival. Lala started his journey from Kabul to come home and spend Eid days with his family and friends. He had his medal of honor with him to show it to his parents and villagers. Lala had earned the trust of Division. He could carry his gun all the time, even if he returned home.

On the eve of Eidi-Qurban, Lala was walking along the Qalai Haji desert. He was close to his village. The solitude of desert and mild winds awakened his memories. Like blossoms of an almond tree, the appealing intrigue faces appeared in front of him. The brave soldier was not afraid of robbers. He walked courageously and without any fear along echoing deserts. The only friend he accompanied during his long journey was his rifle.

Afzal and Agha, the two most dangerous robbers had created fear in rural areas of Kabul. They were brutal and vicious. Government authorities were incapable of dealing with them. They had robbed houses, mugged people and killed dozens of men and women. 100,000 Afghani was posted for anyone who would provide a lead that results in their capture. 60,000 Afghani was posted for anyone who brings their head. In addition, the government had posted the riffles will be awarded to one who provides the information.

Lala always told his friends "It is such a shame that two muggers kill innocent men and women, rob their homes, but there is not one single brave man to stop them and eradicate their fear from public's mind."

Lala missed his parents and he wanted to get home as soon as possible. It was evening and the day was getting dark. Lala performed his evening prayer and headed towards his village through a deep trench. The trench was around 15 meters deep and 20 meters wide like a flooded hole. He had not walked more than a few steps out of the trench when he heard a voice.

"Do not move!"

Lala only listened to his senior officers. He did not pay attention and kept going. The voice was heard again, but this time with anger and rage.

"If you do not stop, I will put a bullet in your head."

The courageous soldier, who had completed similar training and experienced battles, moved quickly, prepared his rifle and created a defense line.

"What do you want?"

"We want your rifle!" This time two voices were heard simultaneously.

Lala replied

"Rifle is government property and my pride."

The men continued

" It is either your life and gun or gun. Haven't you heard our names? I am Afzal and this is my friend Agha."

" If I could recognize that you are who you claim, I will hand over my rifle to you"

The men covered in black clothes like ghosts stood out of caves. Bang…Bang. The sounds echoed in the air and two bodies fell on the ground. Lala walked towards them, grabbed their rifles and continued his journey.

Just a few hundred feet away, Lala heard screams and cries. He saw two passengers tormented and ropes tied up on their feet and hands and left on a desert to die. Lala approached them slowly, loosed their hands and freed them.

Lala arrived home and spent the night at his parents' house. He was happy that he was going to meet the authorities and get the prize. He was very excited that he had freed the public from fear of famous muggers. Lala and his father left home and went to the government office to hand over the guns. Lala saw things differently. Lala did not know the authorities were on Afzal and Agha's payroll.

"Yesterday evening when I was coming home, I encountered two muggers. They identified themselves as Afzal and Agha, and I believe the government had posted award for their capture or death. They attempted to steal my rifle; I had no choice but to kill them."

Authorities who hated Lala and his friends saw this as an opportunity and acted on it. First, they had lost the main source of their income, and second, Lala would have outsmarted the power of authorities in publics' eye. It was too much for the governor to process if they did not use this opportunity as a trap.

Governor changed the narrative. He ordered his officers to arrest Lala and his father. The officers seized Lala's rifle and the rifles he had taken from muggers. The governor notified the Ministry of Interior that his men have captured Lala and have killed two other famous muggers Afzal and Agha. The governor also added in the report "We chased them for nine months, and finally my men were able to kill and capture them yesterday evening. The one we captured is called Lala and he is also a member of the division."

Just one week later, the governor paid his men 60,000 Afghani, while Lala faced an unknown fate.

(25)

A PRISON

The prison located inside a castle guarded by a dark and scary tower. The tower had a tiny gate and it was deeper than actual ground. The castle was like an empty house. If a prisoner died or was murdered by other prisoners, the dead body remained until the next of keen claimed it. The castle was filled with horror and fear and it felt dread even during the daytime. No one could walk in the castle yard alone.

The governor knew Lala had many friends and he was famous for his courage and bravery. He wanted to keep him somewhere far and isolated. Lala was sent to this horrifying prison. The guards chained his hands to his neck, and his feet to a chump (a big piece of wood). They threw him in the castle and locked the gate from outside. The prison cells were built on two sides of the castle gate. Each cell had the capacity for 10 prisoners, but at least in each cell, 30 people lived.

The governor's hatred against Lala was infinite. He made sure there was no further investigation into his case. He wanted him to spend the rest of his life in a prison cell. Two months passed, and no one could investigate or know anything about Lala's fate. He was drowned, bitten and masticated by insects. Torture and torment were common across all prisoners. The prison halls were shorter than the height of an average person, and prisoners often had to bend over to leave their cells. The cells floors were deeper than the actual ground.

Winters were cold and brutal. Cells floor were wet like the kingdom of insects. The halls were tiny and prisoners walked in one line. Waiting in line was harsh for most prisoners. They were sick, hungry and shackled. Many prisoners were chained in pairs.

The bathroom located on a corner of the castle. It had no roof. The walls had aged and collapsed. It looked scary. Prisoners slept over each other to stay warm during harsh winters. Whenever a prisoner got sick, he had to stay in the hall to get better or die from the pain. They did not want other prisoners to get sick. A few could recover from a sickness.

It was painful for those whose friends and relatives were sick and died in front of them while they were chained and could not help. Guards randomly chose prisoners, wiped them until their skin opened and bled. After ruthless torture, worms nested inside their body. Many died of pain and suffering.

The government did not provide any medical treatment or medicine to prisoners. Prisoners barely get some leftovers to survive on. If a prisoner could not find any food, he had to eat someone else's leftover, if anything ever left.

On the corner of the castle, the special room located. It was a room for torturing prisoners. The circus started every night. Guards practiced all forms of cruelty on prisoners, it had become a form of entertainment for them. In winters, the guards tied feet of prisoners on a chump, chained their hands to their neck, put them on one side to freeze up. Later, they throw buckets of water on them. Prisoner fought to avoid getting frozen. When a prisoner was hungry, he could not move and a thick layer of ice was built between his body and the ground. In summers, guards used a different method of torture. They chained a prisoner on the ground for three days and fed them salt to drain water from their body. They even removed prisoners' nails with cutters.

Lala experienced all forms of torture during his time in prison. He was strong and could bear the pain and suffering and fight back to recovery. When his friends learned that Lala is being continuously tortured, they interact with prison guards, bribed them to stop the torture. His father faced a harsh situation. He sold half of his property and bribed authorities to move his son from the horrific prison to a public prison. Lala's friends used everything to make sure the transfer was complete.

When he was transferred to a public prison, he could walk freely inside the prison without chains. He helped other prisoners and cared for their wounds. He was a veteran and knew how to provide medical treatments. Everyone was inspired by his care and dedication. Soon he was surrounded by friends. Whenever a guard wanted to hurt a prisoner, he stood up against them and prisoners lined behind Lala. The governor was promoted to a higher position, but he could not harm Lala anymore. Lala's friends and parents paid everything they had to get him released. Lala was sentenced to five years in prison. He had to spend two years in a castle, and three years in a public prison.

(26)

THE HEART OF A MOTHER

His mom thought she would meet her son on Eid days after a long time. She had prepared lamb and other recipes for his son. She wanted him to invite his friends and they all taste her recipe after a long time. They were far away from home and they missed homemade cuisine. She wanted to see his son wear his medal of honor for his bravery and courage.

Her son had killed two vicious muggers. She was eager to hear how his son spent his time-fighting enemies. The day got darker and night arrived, but she still waited for her son to come home. She never lost hope and barely blinked looking at the door. She could not sleep for the whole night. She turned on a lamp and waited for his son to walk in. It was not just that day, it took days and nights, but poor mother still stared at the door and waited for his son to come home.

First, she thought authorities have sent her son and husband to Kabul to collect the prize. A month passed and she felt something was wrong. She was anxious and worried about the fate of her son and husband. Finally, her husband was released. Lala's friend had bribed authorities to release the old man to spend his last days beside his old woman. His health condition was also getting worse. When her husband brought the horrifying news, it broke her heart. Lala's friends bribed authorities to get his dirty clothes sent home, cleaned up and send them back to him. His mom touched his clothes and smelled pain. The red and black spots on Lala's clothes told different stories. The black spots represented signs of chains, while red spots represented drops of blood. Picturing her son in a horrendous state wounded her the most. She could not imagine what her son was going through.

Spots of blood and chain got wet with her tears before they touched the bucket of water. The poor mother tried many times to see his son, but she never made it. She even went to the prison gate and begged the guards to see her son, but the guards told her that they were specifically instructed to not allow anyone see him. They told her if she brings a letter from governor, they would allow her to see his son, something that was impossible to happen. The grief and sorrow of not being able to see his son, wounded the poor mother to an extent that she got ill and died.

She had instructed her husband to carry her dead body along the prison gate so his son may look at her before she is buried. She asked them if her son got released; tell him to come over her grave, rub remains of my grave on your wounds. I was not able to give him warm kisses on his wounds; my soil will kiss his wounds and comforts him. Lala heard about her mother. Chumps, heavy metals and tortures never broke him, but the shocking news put his back on the ground and broke his heart.

(27)

A MOMENT OF DECISION

The most important moment of a person's life is the moment of decision. The decision that builds a foundation for greatness and nobility. Lala was wrongly imprisoned and he did not want to spend his entire life in a prison cell. He had seen innocent people suffer for standing against injustice and it had kindled a fire of revenge in his heart. His friends kept him posted how people thought about government and the issue of public uprising to topple the government.

Lala strategized an ingenious plan. He met his friends and instructed them to tell his father to sell everything they have and gave the money to prison guards to not shackle his feet at night. The plan worked and guards became friendly to Lala. It was the best time to act. He knew the outcome was very narrow; freedom or death. His friends notified him that the prison gate closes before the sunset, and there is only one guard patrolling the gate. Sky was cloudy and Lala unarmed the guard and walked out of the prison. His friends waited for him outside the prison. Lala and his friends used the dark night to hide in the gardens and left the area when the night was in its climax. Everyone in his village learned that Lala had broken out of the prison. Those who unconditionally loved him and have seen him suffer cheered his freedom.

Tales were told about him. He was on everyone's mind. The young man never gave up. His bravery and courage were incomparable. No one ever defeated him in wrestling. He never showed fear and fought muggers, robbers and criminals. Authorities avoided harassing people of his village, because they knew he would come after them. He was a swordsman, a wrestler, and supporter of infants and widows. He was found in the frontlines of battles, earned medals and had escaped a prison no one dared to try. Lala and his friends were welcomed everywhere. People embraced them, fed them and hid them in their homes.

Lala camped in a haunted valley where barely people could visit. Men from villages came and joined him. He taught them everything about military tactics. He trained them on fire attacks, force concentration, night combat and survival guide. Religious leaders who opposed government orders joined and supported him. Influential leaders found him best suited for leading the nation. Lala had suffered and everyone knew he was innocent. He was a modest man, and he was very aware of the country's situation. He was wanted by the government, but loved by public. He became the Robin Hood of Afghanistan. He was an eagle who had fled a cage.

At nights, he attacked on one government office and in the morning, he attacked on another one. He always overthrew government forces. He was brave and public supported him. People were tired of government orders and needed a new leader. Religious campaigns boosted public's morale to join him.

It was not a fair battle. It was a battle between an entire army vs. a barefoot person who lived among people. The illiterate and unknown soldier stood up against an armed battalion and ended up victorious. Government called on public to not help him, but in return people assisted him. Rich and corrupt officials feared him and sent him money and ammunitions to fight government forces. Authorities feared him more than they feared their own government.

Stories were told about his fight against government forces. His rifle was feared the most, because it defended poor and vulnerable people. He was the essence of a miracle. He was a leader, but he brought bread on his shirt and feed everyone. People prayed for his victory and named him, Servant of God. Elder women fasted and gave charity for his victory. He was people's hero. A famous proverb was told on daily basis. "When people are on your side, God is on your side."

It was an end to misery and oppression. Oppressors, tyrants and dictators kneeled to him. Changes start happening in many places and orders were reversed. People did not like stylish western phrases and idioms. They wanted to hear in plain and simple language from an illiterate person who felt their pain.

No one had forgotten the horrifying old days. Brutalities, corruption, oppression, and division among ethnic groups were still in their memories. The vicious establishments kept people in chain, shot people with rockets, and built light stands from their head. No one knew why they acted so malicious. They needed answers to their questions.

Why one family must govern all the time and force their foolish policies and orders on people? Why people have to pay the price for achieving independence, but King and his family get the credit? Why people are banned from wearing traditional clothes and are forced to wear western clothes? Why the USSR invaded and occupied Islamic nations, but the government of Afghanistan is quiet and ignores it? Why the government changed public holidays from Friday to Thursday and forced people when to work and when not to work? Why religious signs are removed from national flag and it is replaced with signs of mountains and sun? Why authorities divided people across language, sect, and religion? Why in conflicts between King's family and relatives' innocent people are victimized? Why neighboring countries attacked, killed innocent people and partitioned our country, but government is involved in familial conflicts? Why corruption, bribery and nepotism governed the country?

Everyone sought answer to these questions and many fought for it by joining Lala. Public were angry, and when government attempted to be soft and modify orders and policies, people did not listen to them. They believed the tumor in government cannot be cured. People in rural areas already chose the barefoot grape seller as their king and leader.

People stood up against the government and an uprising started everywhere. People had suffered severely and saw it as an opportunity. They could not wait anymore. Opposition started everywhere including Kandahar in the south of the country. A war between government forces and oppositions begun. An angry nation who had suffered oppression, tyranny and injustice for decades flooded with rage from mountains and valleys towards cities. In most cities, they ousted armed forces with stones and sticks.

In Kabul, people asked Lala to lead them. Lala was an experienced warrior and he knew how to fight and dismantle government canons. He was like an eagle in a mountain, a leopard in a desert, and a trained soldier in a battle. Hunger and starvation did not slow him down. He was tortured severally and did not want anyone to suffer anymore.

The government initiated a peace process with Lala, but it was a conspiracy planned by his cabinet to catch and kill him. The peace process failed. Lala visited southern parts of Afghanistan and evaluated the situation. Leaders from north of Kabul met and greeted him. Leaders of Shinwar and Mumand districts in the south agreed to fight against government forces. Authorities saw that government is losing the war; they secretly provided information on government movements.

War moved from rural areas to cities. The capital

was guarded by towers. The King's palace located in Kabul city and it was protected by fearful and world advanced cannons that scared everyone. Kabul city had garrisons in each checkpoint like steel walls. Fighter jets were prepared in airports to counter any threat to the city. They could bombard anywhere anytime. Civilians noticed an increase number of officers in the city. A giant wall separated the city from Khairkhana Bridge to Rafi Tower. It was made of metal and fire, signifying an unshakable power.

The King invited Kazim Padshah, a Turkish military general and famous conqueror to fight against the barefoot grape seller and defeat him. General Padshah prepared an army and planned to attack and end them without giving them a chance of retreat. The plan included infantry, cavalry, cannons and air forces. Date and time for the invasion were set. The night before the invasion, Lala received the news about government forces plan. Lala knew many lives would be lost and the fate of his country would be gambled. He knew that tomorrow his countrymen will fight and die at both sides of the war, and it hurt him more than anything else. Lala an illiterate leader was facing a sophisticated military general.

Lala and his army only had swords, short range riffles and knives, while government forces had advanced weaponries, cannons and airplanes. It was a battle between wealth and poverty, luxury and scarcity. The King, his family and relatives thought they have achieved the independence from colonizers, but people had lost lives. Lala a barefoot grape seller led an army against enemy at home. He was an ordinary person with extraordinary character. He was son of an ordinary person and a grandchild of an ordinary man.

(28)

A DECISIVE DAWN

A glorious and magnificent tower located on the northwest of Hussain Kot Castle. The castle belonged to Mirza Mohammad Hussain, a public accountant at previous King's administration. He was hanged by authorities in the beginning of the Amanullah Khan's reign just twenty kilometers away from his home in front of his children, family and relatives without any trail. All his properties were confiscated. The castle was in the middle of a colorful garden. The surrounding was covered with green lawns, luxuriant trees, and dancing fountains that enchanted viewers in summer and winter. However, that night the entire garden was covered with snow, and one could not spot anything.

Gates were locked from inside. The classical

gasoline lamb lit up halls of the castle with its semi-yellow color. Lala sat in the corner of hall. He was wounded. His left hand was tied to his neck due to injuries. Lala had lost lots of blood and his skin had paled. He had a military uniform and many bullet magazines around his waist. He wore a black leather hat and his tiny turban covered his head to ears. He tied up the other end of his turban to his chain hiding his light beard. His two leopard eyes were visible from distance.

He placed one side of his German manufactured rifle on the ground, while the front side was under his shoulder. The riffle was sent to him by one of King's ministers. Magazines of bullet hung on his leader belt like a fish swimming in a tank. A sharp knife hanged on his waist too. The handle of the knife was made of animal bone and barely visible. The shadow from his big shoulders, and his sprightly body created a formable direst figure on the ground. He stared at his shadow.

Many influential leaders whose parents fought in the war of independence sat around him in a circle. Soldiers stood a few feet away and were prepared to follow orders. The news of the government attack had stunned everyone. Many tribal leaders recommended that they should leave the castle right now and ran away as far as they could. They should hide and when the weather gets better, they may come back and continue the fight. Their fear was real. The weather was cold and they knew that more men would die freezing than in the battle ground. Lala listened to leaders, but he was quiet. Anger and disappointment were visible in his face. The nascent young fighters told Lala if they part, everyone would get captured and killed by government or die of cold weather. We may not make it the season. The consultation took longer than expected. Lala broke his silence and continued.

"God is with us. We will have the victory before dawn."

It was a bold claim! Everyone stared at each other. He knew the moment of decision had arrived. He explained his plan to everyone, opened the gates and walked towards the garden. From the tiny scattered holes in the walls of the castle, it was visible that Lala and his fellow fighters were walking out of the castle.

Everyone performed the night prayer at Murad Baig Mosque, and camped behind the snow-covered mountains of Khairkhana. They had already climbed to the neck of the mountain. It wasn't dawn yet. He saw 20,000 government forces. The camp was dark and silent like a dead desert. Number of tents reached almost three thousand like a crystalline cemetery. Commanders the and generals had gone to the city and left the army without command. It was a perfect moment for Lala to implement his strategy.

Lala and his companion divided into three groups. The first group camped at the right side of the cave of the Khairkhana valley, the second group camped at the left side, and the third group accompanied Lala. Government forces hadn't slept for hours due to cold weather and lack of fuel for warming their tents. Due to corruption, government aid never reached to soldiers. They had to wrap themselves up in their blankets.

"Tomorrow will be a sad day. We will face a dark and tearful fate" government forces whispered to each other.

Does it even worth fighting our own brothers and countrymen for the king? Do we have to follow military generals' orders who kept us in this freezing cold weather thirsty, hungry and cold, while they are in their warm beds. Do we listen to what God inspires or what these luxurious men tell us? Our religious leaders warned us not to fight our countrymen? We all have seen night letters? Why we fight and defend those who make our life worse than hell!

These thoughts bothered most of the soldiers. Many among soldiers worked for Lala and informed him about the situation inside the camp. Lala knew nothing could stop him. He and his rifle men walked towards the camp. The influential leaders who were accompanying him chanted God is great while everyone entered the camp.

The roaring increased and echoed in the camp. Soldiers immediately left their tents and ran out. Lala had given instruction to his men to shoot in the air when the soldiers leave their tent. Chants of God is Great gave everyone Goosebumps. Soldiers felt the entire camp was already under control of Lala. An old man in white with long beard and turban recited verses of holy Book "Quran". The soft voice and the rhythm of the recitation enthralled everyone. When he finished, he addressed soldiers.

"We are not here to rob camp of our brothers. Tonight, the mountain and valleys are safe. God is merciful. We are all together in this. Do you listen to God or you want to listen to your coward commander who is hiding under his blanket? Justice will always prevail and oppressor will always be punished. "

He was not finished, when chants got louder from all corners of the camp. They had strong harmony and it moved the camp. Lala knew it was the time to address his people.

"My dear brothers! I am a simple soldier like every

one of you. I have served my country and my beliefs unconditionally. I have been tortured and oppressed for what I stand for. Today I am in your hand, whatever decision you want to take about my fate, I accept it."

He had not concluded his speech when the morning call for prayer started. Soldiers stood up in two lines next to each other after the old man to perform the Morning Prayer. Prayers in the first line were Lala's men; while prayers in the second line were government forces.

It was still morning and soldiers left the camp. King Amanullah Khan who had gone mad about development after returning from Europe swore his allegiance to his older brother. By noon, the King in his luxurious car left the palace and headed towards Kandahar. Just three days later, the barefoot grape seller entered King's Palace.

(29)

A HUMBLE KING

Enayatullah Khan did not want to be a King, but he agreed to run the country when his younger brother, the King fled the country and left everything in chaos. When his father was assassinated in Laghman province, Enayat left the Kingdom to his younger brother. He was a wise man. He did not like the idea of going into a war against his younger brother for power.

When the King left country unsupervised, Enayat had no choice but to accept the responsibility of holding the nation together. His younger brother, the King and authorities insisted that he must take control of the country.

Government forces still controlled many parts of Kabul. They decided to protect the Palace and the new King against Lala and his army. Government forces had joined Lala after the conciliation in a military camp. The new army under Lala's leadership seized the capital and surrounded the Palace. The new King dispatched a messenger to make peace with Lala. In the meantime, Lala had not yet recovered from wounds he had received during the battle. A Bomb Shrapnel was still in his shoulder. The government forces bombarded Lala's men days before he seized the capital.

The Message from the new King was not delivered to Lala properly. The content was ambiguous and soldiers who had recently joined Lala assumed a conspiracy was in place by Amanullah. Influential leaders who accompanied Lala advised him to not be fooled. Soldiers and generals disagreed with reconciliation, because everyone believed the government wanted to arrest Lala and his friends so they could return back to power. It was something tried many times in the past by the same people.

Public did not want Amanullah anymore. They wanted a new king who loved his people. They wanted a man who respects their tradition, religion and belief. They wanted a simple king, not a luxurious and wasted leader. They needed a king who would fight for them and side with innocent people. Public knew Enayatullah was not a King, he was a temporarily cover up for Amanullah's return.

Enayatullah could not defend the throne. Soldiers were approaching the Palace and country was about to engulf in a bloody war. He recused himself from power and left the country. Soldiers conquered Kabul and hung up Lala's flag on City gates. People played drums and commended a festival. Influential leaders embraced Lala as their King and covered his head with a piece of white cloth instead of a golden crown.

The new King was named "The Servant of God". New coins were minted from silver and gold in recognition of his legitimacy. Lala introduced his ministers and cabinet. People loved the new king. He was brave, courageous and walked among his people like a rural man. A few rich families, who had lost power and wealth due to recent changes, criticized him for being illiterate. Public's response to them was very simple. Literacy is not the only criteria for leading a nation; our prophet was illiterate too. Haters even criticized him that he did not come from a royal family. People responded to them, great empires were built by simple people not royal families.

Father of Jacob Laith, the founder of Samanid Kingdoms was a dish washer. Sabuktigin, father of Sultan Mahmood was a slave. Qutbidin Aybak, emperor of the Indian Territory was bought from a slave market. Nadir Shah Afshin, the founder of

Afsharid dynasty of Persia was a coat maker.

The illiterate grape seller finally achieved something no one ever thought about it. He sat in the throne; a throne whose power reached borders of India and the Central Asian States.

(30)

A COURT HOUSE

It was an early morning. Leafless trees were naked like stripped prisoners in line. The sun shined grey on palace walls. Snow had disappeared from most parts of the city. Residents were eager to meet their brave king. Everyone wanted to know who this strange unknown man was. He had defeated an entire army and dethroned a powerful king with a rifle. Everyone liked him because he belonged to a poor farmer family. Everyone knew he was wrongly imprisoned before and he had spent dark cold nights in horror. He had climbed mountains and camped in valleys to defeat a strong powerful ruler.

Everyone had heard about his courage and bravery.

People gathered in the Palace garden to meet him. It was for the first time the Palace garden was opened to the public. The garden was a luxurious place and only a comfort place for royal families. People also expected to know what will happen to the guards of King; the soldiers who defended Enayatullah Khan and had killed many soldiers. Streets were filled with people. Everyone wanted to get closer. People were tired of wars. They wanted an end to misery and oppression.

People waited impatiently. The time on the tower clock showed 9:00 AM. The King had not arrived yet. An hour and a half passed and the sound of the Iron Gate at the north of the Palace rang. Everyone looked at Iron Gate. Guards of dethroned King were lined up in front of Palace fences. Victorious riflemen circled them to create a distance between the public and guards.

The king's men entered the garden. People kept looking. Influential and tribal leaders followed King's men. Cabinet members walked after them. People were excited, but still impatiently searching for their king. Ex-Military generals and ministers were seated at the left side of the garden, Relatives and family members of Amanullah waited on the stairs of the palace.

Soldiers raised a flag with signs of God is Great.

The flag grabbed everyone's attention. When people looked back to the garden, they saw the servant of God. The King walked alone towards his people. His rifle was on his shoulder. People tried to push away to get closer. Palace servants opened fences on the first floor of the palace.

A man in tanned color appeared in front of the curious and impatient public. He had a wide forehead. His chin appeared like a lion nose but straight. His short beard and big shoulders shaped his appearance like a warrior. Fear and mercy echoed in his face. His grey outfits were covered with steel and iron. Corners of his turban wrinkled like the feather of a bird. His smiles spoke of his nobility and his behavior showed his bigheartedness. His was wounded and could not move his left hand. Officers welcomed the arrival of the King by playing three times a drum. An old man in government employee uniform walked a few steps closer. His hands were shaking. He represented people of Kabul and addressed the audience. He congratulated the king and promised that people are behind their new king. He wished the king success and good health, and hoped peace and welfare for the public.

Sounds of Amin echoed. Lines got tighter and closer. Everyone wanted to see him. Distance between the public and the King got as closer as a few feet. The King addressed his people.

"I am standing here because of god's favor and your support. Our leaders and scholars voted that the wasted king must leave, and I should serve my people. I am the same old farmer. Nothing has changed. I am that illiterate soldier. I hope I could serve you all, and accomplish the promises I made to my God. There is no difference between you people and I. You are all kings."

His simple and humble speech was accompanied by applauses. Now, it was time for avenge and punishment. Punishment for guards of the dethroned king who fought even after the entire government army had surrendered.

Detained guards were brought closer to the King. They expected a certain death. People thought the sword man who was so good at fighting will only think about avenge. A silence-controlled masses. The king continued.

"I love all of you. You all fought with bravery and courage against me. My enemies are those who I have trusted before and they betrayed me. You have killed my friends, and I forgive you on behalf of them. Please forgive my friends who have killed your friends. Forgiveness is an act of a gentle man. If you want to continue your duty, we still need you."

Bravo and hurray echoed.

The guards responded.

"It would be a shame for us if our leader is alive and we serve someone else. We would like to go back to our families."

The King paused for a minute and told them.

"I see bravery and courage in your words. We will pay for your travel expenses. Please send my greetings to your families in Kandahar."

The tower clock hit 01:00 PM. The King walked back towards the palace and the guards closed the gates.

(31)

JUSTICE FOR VICTIMS

There are only two true happiness in life; love and freedom.

Luxurious rooms and offices of the Palace were trampled by rural people. They were not familiar with modernized life style. They sat on a floor and eat with bare hand. They believed knives are for cutting and they did not recognize forks. Their tradition was different. They praised God before the meal and thank him after it. A twenty-four hour was separated into five slices for them. They prayed five times a day. They washed their mouth and teeth five times a day with a tree root. They did not know about toothbrush or toothpaste. They woke up before dawn and went to bed after the night prayer. They were simple. They talked, acted, ate and dressed simple. They were humble. Women in rural areas did not wear scarfs on their head, but when they visited cities, they wore them. Western uniform and dress code were awkward to these farmers. They did not want to have a piece of cloth (tie) on their neck like a chain on a dog.

Proper medicine did not exist. When someone got sick, they turned to traditional herbal medicines. During previous kings, doctors were always sick. Every time they prescribed a medicine to the King or his family, he had to try it first, to prove it that it was not poison. Luxurious life style, expensive appliances and silverwares were surprisingly funny to new residents.

Time flied quickly and a couple of months passed. The Independence Day was close. Royal families were replaced with farmers, but the Independence Day was as important as before to the nation. People had paid in blood for independence. Public hated everything about the previous government, but they still loved the Independence Day.

Every year Independence Day was celebrated in Paghman District of Kabul. It was a place only for rich and elite families. Public could not attend the event. The new king wanted to celebrate the day with his people. He wanted an inclusive celebration for everyone. Advisors chose west of Kabul for the celebration. It was a sacred place for the people of Kabul. A couple of teams were assigned to decorate the place. Public volunteered with passion and appetite. Kabul River was blocked and small boats with colorful lamps were placed on the river. The decoration illustrated victory and triumph.

Old cannons were placed at two sides of Kabul Mountain. The tower of Elm-Jahl; the slaughter house of previous King was covered with black cloth. People were united; there was no south and north and the city bloomed with colors.

The king ordered his people to light up Kasa Burj with candles. He wanted to thank martyrs of wars. It was a heart touching celebration. No discrimination or prohibition existed or allowed. Tents of ministers, military generals and ambassadors were placed around the festival ground. A seat was positioned in the middle of the ground for the King. It was a place where everyone could see him. A barbed wire was extended 200 meters around the king to block people from getting closer to him. A newspaper was found (Habibul Islam) to report on the Independence Day.

Many believed the King should not be available to their people. When a king is kept away from his people, it makes him valuable and classy. In the middle of the barbed wire, a small door was installed for commuting. The seat was three meters high and its steps were adorned with red velvet. Authorities had asked the Minister of foreign Affairs to deliver the king's message. The king was illiterate and had no formal education. His ministers wore suits and tie, while the king himself wore traditional clothes. Former government officials waited impatiently to find a weak point about the king and criticize it, but there was no room for pessimists.

Public embraced the festival with love and passion. People feared that a devilry might happen and ruin their happiness. Joy of love had overcome sought of revenge. The servant of God, the king ordered to free all prisoners who were imprisoned for small crimes in honor of the Independence Day.

Public waited for their King to appear on his throne. The event coordinators announced the king will be joining us at 4 PM and the minister of foreign affairs will address the public on behalf of the King.

It was at 4 PM. A group of musicians played music. Sounds of cannons on both sides of mountain cave shook the ground. People saw a man in simple military uniform, a hat and humble gesture walked towards the throne and greeted them. Unlike Amanullah and previous kings, he had no luxurious ride. He was the king, a son of a water carrier for martyrs and defeater of kings' throne and crowns. When he arrived at his throne, he starred at barbed wires and instead of walking through the door; he jumped over barbed wires like a leopard and commanded his generals.

"I want all these barbed wires removed. I don't want these stuffs to stand between my brothers and me." The king climbed up the stairs swiftly.

He responded to people's applauses, greetings and respect by waving his hands towards them. Thousands of audiences thought that the silver box on the desk will be opened and a letter will be given to the minister of foreign affairs to read the King's message, but unlike expectations, he closed the silver box and in his simplest way said.

"My God has given me the ability to talk, why I should not talk to my people myself…

"Asalamu Alikum,

In the name of God, I congratulate this festival to all of you.

My dear people!

The Independence belongs to all of you. It is not Amanullah Khan's father's heritage neither my old dad's. You all have paid for this in blood. Amanullah has not lost anyone in the war of independence; you have lost your loved ones. Always be brave, courageous, and God will help you keep that honor and pride. I hope that the God lead all of us to prosperity and do not allow our enemy to use this situation against us. Our enemies must know we are united against them."

He finished his words and walked toward the throne while shouts, applauses, and bravos continued. Amir Sayed Aalim, the exiled king of Bukhara and Ibrahim Baig a warrior from Tajikistan accompanied him. He was befriended with Ibrahim Baig in Dushanbe of Tajikistan and he knew Amir Sayed Aalim from Hussain Kot garden when he used to work as a farmer.

The celebration ended with happiness and peace of mind.

The king took part almost in all exhibitions and demonstration. One of influential leader recommended watching conquest of Andalusia, a movie appropriate for the ceremony. The king liked the suggestion.

Among all the competition, throwing arrows was mostly liked by many people. The king was the winner at it. His skills surprised the audience. This was the joy of freedom.

(32)

HAPPINESS OF LOVE

Almost the entire country came under the control of the new government. New reforms and changes occurred in most sectors and areas. Proper documentation processes were needed in government offices. Ministry of Justice was replaced by the office of the supreme judges. Habibul Islam Newspaper was established under the leadership of Burhanudin Kushkaki, a famous writer. Western dress code was replaced by the national dress. Turban defeated hats. The Nation calendar which was replaced by Gregorian returned to the solar calendar. Friday became a holiday again. Schools were closed temporarily due to public appeal. Most of the former government ministers and officials joined the new government.

Hijab became obligatory for women.

Training for military officers started under the command of General Mohammad Sami. General Sami was from Iraq, but he had completed his education in Turkey. Council of Islamic and Public Society was founded under the leadership of Mohammad Aazam Khan. Mohammad was the son of Jalandar Khan Tatmudraia, an influential leader. Members of the council were chosen from patriot personalities including Ghulam Mohammad Khan Wardak (former minister of interior). The minister of foreign affairs was instructed to dispatch representatives to foreign countries for the recognition of the new government.

The office of the king was led by a well-known scholar and writer Sherjan. Titles of Vice-King, and assistance vice-king were created in the administration, but unfortunately, power was in the hands of those who had attended war of victory and most of them were illiterate.

The king little by little got used to habits of palace residents. Sherjan checked orders while the king stamped and approved them. However, orders and decrees that were dispatched to his fellow friends and comrades, Sherjan had no access to them.

He was a brave king and feared no one. He did not need a body guard. His humbleness touched hearts.

He managed military and administration affairs during the day, and went to bed late at night. He was tired and exhausted. The new establishment needed a lot of work. He had his lonely times too. He thought about his childhood and recalled his memories.

He had learned a lot from his father and the stories he had told him. He recalled nights of prison, tortures and punishments he had gone through. He recalled Gul Chehra and how she fed him like a mother. He recalled beautiful mornings of Kalakan, his village. He recalled a beautiful branch of almond tree and memories attached to it.

Royal families in Kabul felt that they were losing power and royalty life. They plotted to trap the king inside Harem. They planned to make a royal daughter the queen to have access in the king's court. They consulted the ministers and brought a proposal to the king. The king accepted the offer, but his heart was stolen by someone else. A single look of an angel face that had sent him a message of love and devotion.

Who could bring the good news, first and last name of that girl? Who would search for her? Gul Chehra was gone and the castle was in chaos. It was a tragedy that only the king felt it. What a senseless love? Secrets of his heart were only known to the breeze of morning and branch of an almond tree. Alas! The breeze cannot talk and the branch of almond three cannot help. He could not share his secret with anyone.

His heart was out of control. He was a prisoner of throne and power. Eyes and ears of enemies and friends were at him. Everyone searched for a negative point to criticize him for it. He talked, walked and behaved like a king, but the feelings in his heart was like a paradise peafowl who wanted to fly with a herd of peafowls and forget kingdom and throne.

If he was that old barefoot grape seller, he could have walked for miles and searched for her. He could have searched villages, towns and cities to find her and no one could have noticed him.

Many weeks passed, and both families met and exchanged gifts. The bride was from a royal family and she could read and write. She was engaged to a king, who could not read and write.

The king had an untamed soul and both families hoped that the bond of the beautiful and wise queen with brave and courageous king will bring peace of mind to the king and soften him. There were bad elements within the administration that could have hurt the king, and wise advisors wanted the king to remove them from power.

The Palace walls were decorated with colorful cresset lights. The bride was inside a cradle made from luxurious items. A Rolls Royce car carried the cradle to the palace. The bride was accompanied by many more cars and loud music. The bride entered the palace from the east gate.

The bride walked inside the hall of fate. Her fate was about to bound with a stranger she had never met. She only knew he was the man who had dethroned a powerful king with a rifle and a sword. A furious warrior who had become a king, but he lived like a regular person. He wore plain clothes and turban. He attended battles every day and never left his rifle on the floor. His chest and warms were covered with magazines full of bullets. His clothes smelled gunpowder and blood. He sat on the floor and ate with his bare hand. He ate everything and never criticized a cook or preferred one food over another one. He was an illiterate, but he stamped on decrees and orders.

The bride sank in thoughts and worries. The groom had a lion heart, but still lived in slumber land. She was about to embed with a stranger, and he was about to share his bed with someone from his enemy's family. The king did not know if she was happy about the bond or not. They had never seen each other and the foundation for this marriage was totally political.

Two birds sat on a throne. Mesmerizing music and lights added color to their feelings. Families of king and bride brought the holy book and mirror of fate. A mirror which groom and bride see each other for the first time.

Family and relatives of the groom were simple and rural families. They had long sleeves, wide skirts and frosty eyes. Families of the bride were stylish and covered in expensive jewelries. It was an awkward moment. Both families sounded bizarre to each other due to their life style and fashion.

The bride's face was covered with a thin silk veil. The groom's family removed the veil and asked the groom to kiss the holy book and look in the mirror. When he looked at the mirror, he felt Goosebumps all over his skin. The feelings touched his soul and his heartbeat increased. He almost exploded from happiness and surprise. It was not a stranger's face. It was the face nailed in his heart, with glances behind a branch of almond three. He saw a bit of sadness and tears in that face.

Days passed and one night in his decorated silky throne three creatures slept. A hero in simple clothes; filled with love, happiness and gratitude. A beautiful innocent girl; in fears and doubts, and a rifle; representing a symbol of courage and righteous. It was a happiness of love.

(33)

THE END OF A JOURNEY

After a couple of months, everything suddenly changed. Young inexperienced fighters who had accompanied the king in the journey to the kingdom wanted partnership in the government affairs. They influenced the administration and interfered in military affairs.

The king wanted to get rid of them, but it was not easy. They pushed away experienced people from government offices and broke all the promises the king has made to his people. The king had regrets about leaving the wrong people in charge and had to face a painful consequence.

Intellectual individuals and personalities were aware of the matter and how serious it was, but they had no power or authority to face them. The bad elements in the administration even canceled development projects and plans. They introduced modernization unreligious and against people's tradition. People were furious and irritated about changes and they did not recognize political plot from injustice.

The king had come to power because the nation wanted him. He did not plan revolution; it was a responsibility he had undertaken to save his people from oppressors. People had shown hatred against the government not for bad laws, but due to bad people implementing the law. Schools were closed and conciliation was voided. Bribe and corruption found its way back into the business. Nepotism governed the administration. Government incomes fell short. Trade and employment were decreased. Conflicts and skirmish over language, ethnicity and religion started again and reached its climax.

The king was left alone. He had his sword and thoughts about how to use them to bring justice. His second in command was a coward. Sayed Hussain was a luxurious man who even slept with more than twenty-five girls at a time. He was often occupied with revelry and debauchery.

Governors and officials became cruel. Injustice and oppression governed cities and people hated the new administration. The king was forced from inside and outside the kingdom. Members of Amanullah administration who resided in foreign countries used this opportunity to provoke people against their king.

Mohammad Sediq, a famous military general who led the national army in Paktia province came under attack. He was wounded and had injuries in his right leg. At this critical time, a global competition between two superpowers increased. The Russian Federation backed Ghulam Nabi Charkhi in Mazar-e-Sharif. He was a military general and a supporter of Amanullah Khan. Russians provided him with air and ground support to create chaos in the north. At the same time, the Great Britain brought Mohammad Nader Khan from France to India. The Great Britain armed Nader Khan and tribal men and sent them to Afghanistan. In Kandahar, Governor Hussain Ahmad khan, a brother in-law of Amanullah Khan declared his kingdom. The king sent his troops to four corners of the country to Mazar, Jalalabad, Kandahar, and Gardiz.

Ghulam Nabi lost the battle in Mazar-e-Sharif and escaped to Samangan province. The Russians army who had come to support Nabi also returned back to their country. Sayed Hussain the second in command who accompanied over 30,000 soldiers stayed in Mazar-e-Sharif and did not return to Kabul. Over 20,000 soldiers stayed in Jalalabad to counter uprising and attacks. More than 25,000 soldiers stayed in Gardiz, Khost and Ghazni provinces and around 10,000 remained in Kandahar.

Mohammad Nadir Khan who was an experienced con used this opportunity and entered Kabul through Do-Bandi Valley. He could not directly confront the king's army and he knew all the soldiers were dispatched to the provinces.

People were tired of civil wars and wanted stability and peace. The king's few battalions were outnumbered by heavy artillery and foreign army.

Nadir's men attacked Kabul with cannons from two sides of Kabul Mountain. The King asked his men to take shelter in the palace to avoid civilian casualties. Nadir Khan's family was also in the palace. The queen was responsibility for making sure Nadir's family was safe during the conflict.

Nadir feared that the King's soldier soon will arrive from provinces and counter him. He ordered his men to bombard the city without any mercy and kill everyone including his family. Ammunition depot inside the palace was hit with cannons and exploded. Heavy dark smokes created a screen over the palace and surrounding areas. Nadir continued firing cannons and mortars, but the brave and courageous soldiers with all causalities and losses did not surrender.

(34)

THE FINAL NIGHTS

The Palace was under siege from four corners. Nadir's cannons kept coming nonstop. Explosions inside and outside the palace had made it difficult to breath. The city was on fire, but still no news of surrender. Nadir's men brought Akram, a famous mugger and a relative of Agha and Afzal, the two famous muggers killed by the king. They wanted to provoke the king to come out of the palace so they could kill him.

Akram found a way to get closer to the palace fences. He yelled

"Why are you hiding among women?"

The king told his men

"I cannot watch this nonsense. Open the gate"

The king walked through the northern gate and yelled at Akram

"Here I am."

Akram reached for his gun and tried to shoot the king. The king was faster and shot him quickly. Akram fell off the fence. The bang of his rifle echoed in ruins. The king walked back to the palace and his men closed the gate. Nadir's men were dumbfounded by his surprise.

The fight continued for the second night. The king told his men.

"I must find a way for the queen to leave the palace. I will not allow my dignity and pride on the street like Nadir."

The king went to his queen and asked her.

"What do you want my love?"

The queen responded.

"I want to remain next to you until my last breath"

The king insisted and persuaded her to leave the palace with four of his trusted men. He asked her to go to her father's home until things get back to normal.

The king had not slept for days. He asked one of his generals to take the lead so he could sleep for a couple of hours. He walked towards his bedroom. He starred at his men from the window of his room. In every corner of the palace, a body had rest in peace. Many soldiers had died holding their rifle. The enemy had blocked the flow of water to the Palace. The palace had run out of food. Two thousand soldiers were fighting against ten to fifteen thousand soldiers.

The king had lost many men. Only less than three hundred men were alive. More than half of the palace walls were destroyed by explosions and fires.

Four men in black accompanied the queen out of the palace. They had black turbans like the enemy and were barefoot. They used the secret passage of the palace. The queen and four men walked for hours until they reached safety. It was a dark and terrifying night.

The queen was as brave as her husband. She had learned bravery and courage from her king. Death crept everywhere. The queen was fearless.

The queen arrived at her father's house and her family opened the gate. The king had asked her queen to hand over her ring as the sign of her safe arrival.

One of the men approached the queen and extended his hand to get the ring. The queen was about to hand over her ring, when he grabbed her hand. She reached for her pistol to shoot the man, when the man in black whispered to her.

"don't be afraid. God will keep you safe. It is me, my love" the king gave her a warm kiss.

The queen was in tears and told to her king.

 "God be with you my hero and brave husband"

Guards closed the gate and the king listened to his queen's footsteps. The king headed back to his palace. The hope was diminished for the king and his soldiers, but still, they did not surrender.

Nadir could not breach the palace, but instead, he tried to make peace with the king. He promised that the king and his companions can leave through the northern gate and no one will fire or stop them.

The king after nine months of leading the nation walked through the northern gate with his seventeen men and arrived at the Palace of Jabulul Siraj. He waited for his second in command, Sayed Hussain to dispatch his army, but he did not know the coward had already surrendered and sent his son for forgiveness to Nadir.

(35)

A PROMISE

The young and mighty grape seller who had dethroned a powerful king had an assurance that he would continue his struggle and govern for years. Like an angry wounded eagle, he returned to his nest and remained in the Jabulul Siraj palace beneath the snow-covered mountains. His palace was a stronghold and no one could defeat him. He waited for his army to return, so he could fight back against Nadir, but he did not know that his coward vise-king had already surrendered.

He could not believe he was not the king anymore. It was easy for him to forget the pain and suffering of prison, but it was not easy to let go of the responsibility of leading his people. He did not know that people lie and break their promises and he should have not trusted them.

The same men who had come to him and brought the message of Amanullah's surrender came to the king with a holy book and a letter from his queen. Nadir and his men had signed in the pages of a holy book that they will not hurt the king and his men. Nadir and his men had also faked a letter that it was sent by his queen. The letter asked Lala, the king to come to Kabul.

The king entered Kabul. Nadir waited for him in the hall of kings with his ministers and generals. It was an interesting eye-catching moment.

Nadir had a black and white beard and shiny sunglasses. He wore luxurious turban made of French silk. He was born in an elite family. He knew diplomacy. He was a skilled deceitful. The king walked with his men without fear and stood in front of Nadir.

He had trusted Nadir and had come to make peace to end civil wars. He could have become a headache for Nadir for years, but he thought about his people and country. He was calm and quiet, but his eyes shined an eagle. He did not believe that Nadir was a king, he believed the real king is his God. Men come and go.

Nadir asked him to sit down, but he did not follow his order. Everyone was shocked. His nobility and decency shamed all officials. No one could make an eye contact with him. Deceptive glances from shiny sunglasses of Nadir sent him a message. The nobleman was trapped.

The king walked with serenity and took the King's stamp and left it on Nadir's table and continued.

"Dear God,

You are the witness that when my country was at risk from all sides, this illiterate grape seller had to stood up and take care of it. Now I am handing it over to Nadir in good health. I believe it was what you wanted. I hope one day he hands it over to another child of this country without any damage.

The king addressed to Nadir Khan,

"Be careful of these people. They always say "Yes sir, Yes Sir". Stay away from them. They betrayed Amanullah, they betrayed me and they will betray you too.".

When he finished his speech, he turned around and looked at one of the ministers and asked him.

"Isn't that right?"

He told the truth and the truth affected everyone.

The minister could not control himself. He stood up and kneeled with his hands on his chest and confirmed.

"Yes, Sir, that is the truth".

Lala felt he was still the king. Probably it was the last smile on his lips.

The king continued.

"About the fate of my friends, you are not a butcher to kill them. You are not a trade man to sell them. Maybe you are a nobleman and you will keep your promise. About my fate, I have no wish. You can kill me.

(36)

A BUTCHER'S HOUSE

One week passed and the king was imprisoned in the palace with his loyal friends. Sayed Hussain, his second in command and the fool was also imprisoned. He surrendered the king's army to Nadir to make him happy. He was embarrassed and ashamed.

Lala's brave generals all had sacrificed their life for the cause. Trees in the garden had turned yellow. The palace of the queen was quiet and lifeless. The clock on the tower of the palace narrated tale of the day.

The palace and beautiful garden appeared like a butcher's house. Nadir and his men had slaughtered the king and his men on the corner of the northern gate. Son of Ghulam Nabi, a well-known military general was butchered in front of two crystal sculptures of lions. It was a doomed palace.

Sardar Nasrullah Padshah, whose kingdom only lasted three days was buried. In the middle of the garden, Mohammad Nadir Shah bled to death by Abdul Khaliq. Finally, Mohammad Daoud, the founder of Republic System in Afghanistan was killed by Russian puppets inside this palace and his blood mixed up with other innocent martyrs.

Was this a butcher's house or house of a human?

Sher Jan and his brave brother General Mohammad Sediq Khan was also buried in the garden. Once upon a time, their family members wanted to remove his body from the garden and bury them somewhere else. However, his mother, a daughter of Abdul Karim Kohistani said to her people.

"Be careful to not move my sons' body. They rest with their comrades. When a lion dies, he does not need to be buried anywhere specific, because the whole kingdom belongs to him.

Wednesday, April 25, 1980

New Jersey, U.S.A

Khalili

www.ingramcontent.com/pod-product-compliance
Lightning Source LLC
Chambersburg PA
CBHW051114050726
47592CB00002B/824